NARCISSIST NATION

Other works of interest from St. Augustine's Press

George J. Marlin, *The American Catholic Voter: 200 Years of Political Impact*

George J. Marlin, *Squandered Opportunities: New York's Pataki Years*

George J. Marlin, *Fighting the Good Fight: A History of the New York Conservative Party*

St. Augustine, *On Order [De Ordine]*

Karel Wojtyła [Pope John Paul II], *Man in the Field of Responsibility*

Charles P. Nemeth, *Aquinas on Crime*

Philippe Bénéton, *The Kingdom Suffereth Violence: The Machiavelli / Erasmus / More Correspondence and Other Unpublished Documents*

Gerhart Niemeyer, *The Loss and Recovery of Truth: Selected Writings*

Gerhart Niemeyer, *Between Nothingness and Paradise*

Leo Strauss, *Xenophon's Socrates*

Leo Strauss, *Xenophon's Socratic Discourse*

Pawel Armada and Arkadiusz Górnisiewicz, eds., *Modernity and What Has Been Lost: Considerations on the Legacy of Leo Strauss*

Joseph Cropsey, *On Humanity's Intensive Introspection*

Francis J. Beckwith, Robert P. George, & Susan McWilliams, eds., *A Second Look at First Things: A Case for Conservative Politics*

Roger Scruton, *The Meaning of Conservatism*

Paul M. Weyrich and William S. Lind, *The Next Conservatism*

John C. Calhoun, *A Disquisition on Government*

Ralph C. Hancock, *Calvin and the Foundations of Modern Politics*

Robert Hugh Benson, *Lord of the World*

Peter Augustine Lawler, *Homeless and at Home in America: Evidence for the Dignity of the Human Soul in Our Time and Place*

Rémi Brague, *Eccentric Culture: A Theory of Western Civilization*

Jacques Maritain, *Natural Law: Reflections on Theory and Practice*

James V. Schall, *The Regensburg Lecture*

James V. Schall, *The Modern Age*

Marc D. Guerra, ed., *Jerusalem, Athens, and Rome: Essays in Honor of James V. Schall, S.J.*

Leszek Kolakowski, *My Correct Views on Everything*

René Girard, *A Theater of Envy: William Shakespeare*

C.S. Lewis and Dom Giovanni Calabria, *The Latin Letters of C.S. Lewis*

Narcissist Nation
Reflections of a Blue-State Conservative

George J. Marlin

St. Augustine's Press
South Bend, Indiana

Manufactured in the United States of America

1 2 3 4 5 6   16 15 14 13 12 11

Library of Congress Cataloging in Publication Data
    Marlin, George J., 1952–
        Narcissist nation: confessions of a blue-state
        conservative / George Marlin.
            p. cm.
    Includes index.
    ISBN 978-1-58731-565-7 (hardbound: alk. paper) – ISBN
        978-1-58731-566-4 (pbk.: alk. paper) 1. Conservatism–
        United States. 2. Catholics – Political activity – United
        States. 3. Christianity and politics – United States. 4.
        United States – Politics and government – 2009– I. Title.
    JC573.2.U6M352 2011
    320.520973 – dc22   2011013870

∞ The paper used in this publication meets the minimum requirements of the American National Standard for Information Sciences – Permanence of Paper for Printed Materials, ANSI Z39.48-1984.

ST. AUGUSTINE'S PRESS
www.staugustine.net

My efforts are dedicated to

William F. Buckley Jr.,

(1925–2008)

"I should sooner live in a society governed by the first two thousand names in the Boston telephone directory than in a society governed by the two thousand faculty members of Harvard University."

W.F.B. Jr., 1962

TABLE OF CONTENTS

ACKNOWLEDGMENTS

It's not easy being Catholic and conservative in secular "Blue State" New York. Therefore, I am most grateful to these friends and colleagues who "fight the good fight" alongside me: Brad Miner, Michael Crofton, Pat Foye, Robert Royal, and Michael Uhlmann. I am especially grateful to my wife, Barbara, who put untold hours into assembling the manuscript. As with my earlier books, without her efforts, this work would never have been completed.

Parts of this book previously appeared in *The New York Post*, TheCatholicThing.com, *Long Island Business News*, *Human Events*, and *Newsmax*.

I alone am responsible for any errors, inaccuracies or follies in what follows.

George J. Marlin
Nassau County, New York
February, 2011

Chapter 1

America's New Elites: Narcissists

Throughout the history of mankind, every society has had a subset of people who viewed themselves as superior to the rest of the population due to their self-perceived distinctive qualities: intelligence, breeding, class or wealth. These elites have generally held that because they are exceptional persons they are best suited to conduct the affairs of state. C. Wright Mills, author of the critically acclaimed *The Power Elite*, defined these elites "in terms of power – those who occupy command posts." Sociologist Tom Bottomore, in his work *Elites and Society* agreed that "the power elite decides all important issues and keeps the masses quiet by flattery, deception and entertainment."

The ideological formulas of these elites may vary but their ends have been the same – the domination of the common man. These self-proclaimed "managers of the collective life" expect the people to submit to their notions of the good society. For them, "government by the people" has been merely a slogan to humor the masses.

The United States has not been exempt from elitism. Our Founding Fathers debated as to whether an elitist ruling class should oversee the federal government they devised.

Thomas Jefferson was opposed to an artificial aristocracy which was determined by birth and wealth. He preferred a republican hierarchy, a natural aristocracy, whose qualifications would be based on virtue and wisdom which Jefferson defined "as the love of the laws of our country. As such love requires a constant preference of public to private interest."

To produce a natural aristocracy, "a pool of superior minds" from which the people could choose their leaders Jefferson advocated the creation of an educational system that had rigorous standards.

In defense of his position, Jefferson remarked to George Washington, "I hold it to be one of the distinguishing excellences over hereditary succession, that the talents which nature has provided in insufficient proportion, should be selected by the society, that this should be transmitted through the loins of knaves and fools (i.e., monarchs), passing from the debauches of the table to those of the bed."

Jefferson's greatest foils in the early days of the Republic were John Adams and Alexander Hamilton, both of whom preferred a strong-centralized government managed by a very different aristocracy from Jefferson's.

Adams, who was accused of being a monarchist and was often referred to as the Duke of Braintree, believed Americans should be governed by an aristocracy defined by birth and wealth. "There are few in whom" Adams wrote in his *Defense of the Constitution of the United States*, "all these advantages of birth, fortune and fame are united . . . the natural aristocracy . . . forms a body of men which contains the greatest collections of virtues and abilities."

As for Hamilton, Jefferson claimed he "was not only a monarchist but for a monarchy bottomed on corruption." Hamilton dismissed Jefferson's agrarian politics as a sham; the musings of a Virginia aristocrat who loves the small farmer in the abstract. Instead he called for an elite that would be powerful enough to check "the turbulent and uncontrollable masses"; to keep "the imprudence of democracy on a leash."

Hamilton had a Hobbesian, cynical view of man. He said, "Every man ought to be supposed a knave and to have no other end, in all his actions, but private interest. By this interest, we must govern him and, by means of it, make him cooperate to public good, not withstanding his insatiable avarice and ambition."

To achieve this end, Hamilton preferred a strong central government that would curb the narrow-minded actions of the individual states. He also supported a Senate with life tenure populated by an elite, not of self-righteous members of the land-gentry (i.e., Jefferson) but an elite of strong-willed men who were motivated by self-interest.

The Jeffersonians versus the Federalists was not the only battle over the role of elites in American life. Over time there have been political parties or organized groups that have embraced the elitist notion that the people cannot be relied on to govern themselves hence the best political structure is an efficiently engineered society. As Jeffrey Bell writes in his 1992 work *Populism and Elitism*, "Pessimism about people's ability to do well at [governing] leads to a belief that the people should delegate the setting of standards to various elites, elected officials or more often in recent years, judicial and bureaucratic elites appointed by the elected officials and accountable only tenuously to the people."

In 19th and early 20th centuries, America's elitist groups included the Whigs, liberal-Republicans, progressive-Republicans, "Good-Government" reformers, Prohibitionists and immigration restriction proponents. In the post-World War II era, the Democratic Party, which was historically the defender of the common man – farmers and laborers – emerged as the home of elitist social engineers. These reform Democrats embraced as their hero Adlai Stevenson of Illinois because he was, according to political analyst Michael Barone, "the first leading Democratic politician to become a critic rather than a celebrator of middle-class culture – the prototype of the liberal Democrat who would judge ordinary Americans by an abstract standard and find them wanting. His cultural elitism and contempt for blue-collar workers engendered a new generation of political progeny who grew up not with the fragmented local politics, which Franklin Roosevelt had grown up with, but instead with the centralized national politics which had grown up with the large central government produced by Roosevelt's New Deal and wartime policies."

That new generation of political progeny would include hundreds of thousands of the sons and daughters of America's "Greatest Generation," who invaded the college campus in the 1960s.

The "Me" Generation Narcissists

The post-war GI Bill of Rights permitted millions of veterans to advance far beyond their forebears' achievements. By acquiring a college degree or the skills to enter a trade and to obtain a federal housing loan, they were on their way to entering the ranks of the nation's middle-class. And to achieve that American dream they were committed to family, church, discipline, sacrifice, loyalty and hard work.

Because these Americans, who became the parents of the seventy-six million baby boomers born between 1946 and 1964, survived the horrors of war and the Great Depression, they wanted their children to be brought up in an environment of plenty. Baby boomer parents worked hard so their children could grow up in fine homes in the suburbs, not coldwater flats in the inner city. Their children were to be dressed in the latest fashions, not hand me downs. They were to have the newest toys and they were to receive the best education. Their children were to have all the material goods and advantages they were denied in their youth.

Many of these parents, however, overindulged their children. They showered them with material goods but failed to instill in them the work ethic they practiced, that every right has a corresponding responsibility, and they failed to teach them the greatness of America and its institutions.

These children came to believe that success meant having plenty of objects – big homes, expensive cars, the latest gadgets. It did not mean earning respect by achieving worthy goals through dedication and hard work. Material benefits, comforts, and security were viewed as entitlements, not privileges. They never learned tolerance or patience – they expected special considerations and instant gratification and were petulant and self-righteous. They gave rise, social-philosopher Christopher Lasch wrote, "to the narcissistic culture of our time which . . . translated the predatory individualism of the American Adam into a therapeutic jargon that celebrates not so much individualism as solipsism justifying self-absorption as 'authenticity' and 'awareness.'"

In the 1960s, the impatient members of this generation hit the college campuses. When World War II commenced, there were 1.3 million students enrolled in colleges and universities; by 1968 that number had swelled to 6.9 million. And unlike their parents who matured before entering the ranks of academia, by leading battalions into battle or commanding flying squadrons, and were trying to make up for lost time, these twenty-something pampered kids, observed cultural historian Klaus Fischer, had the leisure "to break the generational ties that usually safeguard historical continuity."

They were to become members of the "me" generation a/k/a narcissists who had grandiose views of their talents, excessive interests in themselves, a craving for attention and admiration and a consciousness of superiority. This type of narcissist, according to Lasch, "depends on others to validate his self-esteem. He cannot live without an admiring audience. . . . For the narcissist, the world is a mirror, whereas the rugged individual saw it as an empty wilderness to be shaped to his own design." Success for these narcissists "consists of nothing more substantial than a wish to be vastly admired; not for one's accomplishments, but simply for oneself, uncritically and without reservation."

These "me generation" kids, estimated to be about 10 to 15 percent of America's college population in the sixties, were alienated from the mainstream because they were different;

they were special, superior and enlightened. Hence the old rules of civility and patience did not apply to them; they had to be gratified now. Self-fulfillment had to be immediate. The problems that perplexed man through the ages had to be solved immediately. *The Little Red Book*, authored by one of history's most ruthless mass murders, China's Mao Tse-tung, was a best seller on campuses because its fortune-cookie like bromides solved the need for instant answers that did not require reflection. Harvard professor Daniel Patrick Moynihan, reacting to the shallowness of the students of that time, wrote they were "persons who had apparently scarcely had an adult conversation in their full four years."

The most radical became student activists – members of "the movement" or the "New Left." Starting with the 1964 campus free speech movement through the student anti-war riots at the 1968 Chicago Democratic Convention and culminating in the campus shutdowns opposing Nixon's Vietnam policies, this student revolution was driven by emotions and slogans, not reasoning or scholarship.

These self-righteous student radicals, who had draft-exemptions and continued to accept living allowances and tuition from their much despised middle-class parents, claimed they were the champions of the "powerless," laborers and the poor – groups they never encountered during their sheltered, suburban and gated-community youth. They condemned the American system, as immoral, oppressive, evil and they were convinced they were the anointed ones destined to restore peace and beauty to the United States. They were similar to the early twentieth century European youth movement which the legendary Austrian economist Ludwig von Mises described as "turbulent gangs of untidy boys and girls" declaring that "all preceding generations . . . were simply idiotic [and] henceforth the brilliant youths will rule. They will destroy everything that is old and useless, they will reject all that was dear to their parents, they will substitute new real and substantial values and ideologies for the antiquated and false ones of capitalist and bourgeois civilization, and they will build a new society of giants and supermen."

Social critic Roger Kimball described them more succinctly as "of the privileged, by the privileged, for the privileged."

Students who marched on campus administration buildings did not seek meaningful dialogue, but instead shouted obscenities and made ridiculous non-negotiable demands. And when these rebels did not get their way, they reacted emotionally and many turned to violence. Organized chaos was the order of the day: Deans were locked in their offices, professors were harassed, classes were boycotted, research centers were vandalized, and buildings were torched. Breaking the law was permissible because it was free of self-interest and in the name of "conscience" (which was not properly formed) but used merely as an excuse for license – the right to do what is irresponsible. The radicals behind this upheaval, concluded liberal columnist Chris Hedges, were "infected with the lust for violence, quest for ideological purity, crippling paranoia, self-exaltation, and internal repression as the state system they defied."

At the 1968 Democratic Convention, these same student protestors turned to the streets in the name of liberty and justice after the duly-elected delegates voted down the anti-Vietnam War plank. Because the police were viewed as barriers, it was permissible to taunt and attack the PIGS. Journalist Theodore H. White, observing the "bloody climax," saw "the black flags of the anarchists; Viet Cong flags; red and blue banners; Omega banners; no American flags" as the kids wreaked violence and looted.

The student anti-war movement continued into the first Nixon term with marches on Washington and campus shutdowns (often during final exam week). These narcissists continued to discredit the existing order, had dripping contempt for those who disagreed, sneered at people who were patriotic and supported the men dying in faraway battlefields, and believed they, not the establishment, were really in the know. In November 1969, for instance, when polls showed that 68 percent of Americans supported Nixon's speech on Vietnam, the spokesman for the Harvard Moratorium rejected the possibility saying, "What Nixon has tried to show is that there is a silent majority behind him. We know better."

But narcissists have short-attention spans. They get bored and move on to the next fad or cause célèbre. And so it was with the student peace movement, particularly after the draft was ended in 1973; some decided to drop out of society and lead hedonistic, purposeless lives. They embraced the teachings of Dr. Timothy Leary: "Turn On, Tune In, Drop Out." This meant pursuing free love and illicit drugs which provided immediate thrills. Others, however, pursued careers attractive to elitists: journalism, academics, publishing, the law, community organizing; and they begat a new generation of narcissist elites.

The Millennium-Narcissists

As the narcissists of the sixties generation grew older, they tossed their granny glasses, cut their hair and joined the ranks of the professional and managerial elites who defined themselves by their intelligence. They might still hate "the system" but rationalized that they were using it in order to obtain the power and wealth necessary to promote and finance their radical causes – feminism, environmentalism, one-world government, etc.

These narcissists isolated themselves with like-minded people in the fashionable intellectual neighborhoods in America's metropolitan regions. Whether it was in Manhattan's West Side, Brooklyn Heights or Chicago's Hyde Park, this emerging class glorified experts ridiculed the working class and vilified the electoral process because their rigid ideologies were often rejected at the ballot box.

For instance, in 1977 when New York City's Democratic primary voters chose blue-collar Mario Procaccino as their mayoral standard bearer against the incumbent, Mayor John

V. Lindsay, the elites lost it. Howling that their party was captured by the forces of hatred, fear and negativism, they flocked to the Lindsay camp. These elitist snobs deserted Procaccino because he defended the old neighborhood way of life, "the way of life" *The New York Times* reported, "mocked by Woody Allen at a Lindsay gala when the comedian talked of Mario in his undershirt, drinking beer and watching Lawrence Welk on television," Also there was outright bigotry against inner-city Italians like Procaccino. Even *The New York Times* reported on the issue:

> There is a bias of the upper-middle-income liberal intelligentsia against the lower-middle class, particularly against Italians. You don't read much about that in this country (working people don't write books), but there are Italian jokes and there was a piece in the small *New Journal* at Yale: "The hidden, liberal-radial bigotry toward the lower-middle class is stinking and covered," wrote Michael Lerner, a graduate political-science student and son of columnist Max Lerner. When a right-wing Italian announced for Mayor in New York, a brilliant professor in New Haven said: "If Italians aren't actually an inferior race, they do the best imitation of one I've seen." Everyone at the dinner table laughed. He could not have said that about black people if the subject had been Rap Brown.

In 2009, *The Wall Street Journal* interviewed notable boomers who admitted they were embarrassed by their generation. Mitch Daniels, the governor of Indiana, said they were "self-absorbed, self-indulgent and all too often just plain selfish." *New York Times* columnist, Thomas Friedman, described his generation as "the grasshopper generation eating through just about everything like hungry locusts."

These narcissists who despised people outside their circles and subscribed to a nihilistic ethics of self-esteem that submits to no sapient higher than themselves, brought into the world progeny who were expected to be intellectually, physically and aesthetically superior to the rest of society. James Davison Hunter of the University of Virginia Institute for Advanced Studies in Culture, has written that in America, "nihilism of this kind tends to foster a culture of banality that is manifested as self-indulgence, acquisition for its own sake, and empty spectacle that makes so much of popular culture and consumer culture trivial."

Because these parents rejected the rules of self-restraint they were forced to abide by as youths, they decided to be their children's friends, not authority figures. This "child-centered parenting" caused parents to avoid confrontation, excuse bad behavior, shield their children from unpleasant situations, constantly tell them they were wonderful or brilliant, be overly protective, withhold censorious judgments and to seek their children's approval. "Adults," wrote Diana West in *The Death of Grown-Ups*, "were orbiting around their children rather than the other way around."

Critic Malcolm Crowley in *Exile's Return* held that these hipster parents subscribed to "the idea of salvation by the child" whereas "the world will be saved by this new free generation. [Hence] children [were] encouraged to develop their own personalities, to blossom freely like flowers." This "cult of the self" philosophy, Crowley concluded, promoted the belief that "the body is a temple in which there is nothing unclean, a shrine to be adorned for the ritual of love" and therefore "every law, convention or rule of art that prevents self-expression or the full enjoyment of the moment should be shattered and abolished."

Too many of these parents, wrote Dr. Jean Tracey, author of *The Narcissism Epidemic*, "made the mistake of idealizing their children instead of truly loving them." Children were not steeped in the traditional moral values and codes of modesty, orderliness and respect for authority that guided earlier generations. They were not taught that there is more to life than achieving material comforts, that for every action there are consequences, and that they should not be self-indulgent. "Stay busy and don't hurt yourself" was the golden rule to getting through their youth.

Parental narcissism rubbed off on many of the 50 million millennial generation; kids who are today between the ages of 18 and 30. The children of parents who received Botox treatments, tummy-tucks or plastic surgery, expected the same. For sweet sixteen birthdays or high school graduations, many girls received a breast augmentation or nose surgery. Like their parents, they also expected to be the constant center of attention. Fame was a right as was not ever having one's feelings hurt. The Internet's "My Space" and "Facebook" further promoted their narcissism. Reacting to all this self-absorption, NBC's Brian Williams said "The danger is that we miss the next great book or the next great idea, or that we will fail to meet the next great challenge . . . because we are too busy celebrating ourselves and listening to the same tune we already know by heart."

These self-absorbed, self-centered children grew up in an environment where they were not judged or evaluated, never learned to live with disappointment and became accustomed to receiving praise regardless of their efforts. "Feeling good is more important than performance or achievement," is the maxim by which they have lived. Competition is no longer emphasized because if one is not always the top performer, one's self-respect might be diminished. There are no losers, everyone is a winner. This form of narcissism became big news in December 2006 when *Time* magazine named "You" as the Person of the Year. "The most capricious modern entitlement," wrote George Will, "is self-esteem. . . . So *Time's* cover features a mirror-like panel. The reader . . . can gaze at the reflection of his or her favorite person."

Many competitive games have been eliminated in school gym classes because children get upset if they lose. Gym classes no longer play team games so no one is hurt for being the last picked. Tag and dodge ball are not played because being "it" or singled out to be hit by a ball might diminish a student's self-esteem. To ensure that the results of organized games are equal, scores are often not kept and all players get season-end trophies for participating.

Maintaining the self-esteem of these "trophy kids" at all costs has also impacted school curriculums. Standards have declined, less course and homework is required. Teachers using red ink to critique student work is considered harsh treatment. Study periods have been eliminated in many schools because it limits freedom to choose study time. All opinions are treated equally; there are no valuable or superior ideas, cultures or philosophies. The young narcissists are equal to their teachers and, therefore, free to express themselves at any time in the classrooms.

Teachers expect less work and students expect easy grades. Students hardly ever fail and "B" is the standard grade one gets for showing up. Parents believe that paying tuition means their children are entitled to get good grades. And parents and students will badger teachers at school and at their homes if a grade does not meet their grandiose expectations. The end results: grades are up and SAT scores are declining.

America's universities have also been impacted by the attitudes of the coddled generation. Students struggle to get into Ivy League colleges not for the education, but for narcissist networking or as a "holding pattern until they get on with their lives."

"Universities," Chris Hedges observed, "no longer train students to think critically, to examine and critique systems of power and cultural and political assumptions, to ask the broad questions of meaning and morality once sustained by the humanities." Standards have been dropped to maintain students' self-esteem. The grading curve is no longer a range from A to F, but A to B. Some higher learning institutions have dropped the "F" grade because to receive it is demeaning. One Ivy League school has seven valedictorian speeches to avoid singling out one student as the best. The distinguished political philosopher, Dr. Harvey Mansfield of Harvard tortures his students by giving two grades: the one he must give them and the one they deserve. The *Financial Times* reported "A recent meta-analysis found that between 1982 and 2009 there was a dramatic increase in narcissistic personality traits among college students – in part characterized by an inability to take the perspective of others, a dependence on others for affirmation and valuing oneself regardless of real achievements while seeking constant praise."

The real problems begin, however, when the Trophy Kids complete their schooling. Having been kept busy with music, tennis and yoga lessons for twenty plus years, some look upon young adulthood as their adolescence period. They move back home, expect parents to support them, become perpetual graduate students or backpack through Europe for several years. (*The New York Times* reported in December 2010 that a growing number of high school graduates are taking off a year before starting college to get over the alleged stress.) Others who begin the search for a job have incredible expectations. Having been pampered all their lives and having received inflated feedback and excessive praise, they have incredible self-confidence that borders on arrogance and they expect to instantly achieve status, security and all the material comforts to which they have been accustomed. *Wall Street Journal* senior economic writer for the editorial page summed up the Trophy Kids this way: "My parents' generation lived in fear of getting polio; many boomers lived in fear of getting sent to Vietnam; this generation's notion of hardship is TiVo breaking down."

The days of the employer determining if the prospective employee is suitable for the corporation or firm is over. Today's narcissists determine if the company is suitable for them. "Almost universally they want to find a job that's not just a job but an expression of their identity, a form of self-fulfillment," says Clark University psychology professor Jeffrey Jensen Arnett, author of *Emerging Adulthood*. They expect an entrée level job to pay lots of money, have flexible hours, casual dress codes, plenty of vacation, perks, and to be secure and fulfilling. The job cannot interfere with their personal life or weekend plans so overtime to meet deadlines is a no-no. A 2007 survey revealed that 87 percent of corporate managers agreed that young workers "feel more entitled in terms of compensation, benefits and career advancement than older generations." *Washington Times* columnist Diana West, noted that what these kids lack "is an appreciation for what goes along with maturity; forbearance and honor, patience and responsibility, perspective and wisdom, sobriety, decorum and manners – and the wisdom to know what is 'appropriate' and when."

From day one on the job, the young narcissist is an employer's nightmare. These over-indulgent, cocky children of privilege reject command management. They are colleagues of bosses, not subordinates and assume everyone can be addressed by their first names. They have trouble adjusting to the work world because they expect to get immediately whatever they want. They become emotional and irrational and lash out at co-workers or supervisors when events don't go their way. Since they are not accustomed to being held personally responsible for their actions, job setbacks are, therefore, the fault of others, never themselves. Jeffrey Pfeffer, author of *Power: Why Some People Have It—and Other's Don't*, has concluded that these young executives are incapable of understanding that "success requires ambition, drive and the persistence and resilience to overcome setbacks and to work constantly on weaknesses."

Craving for recognition, these praise junkies demand constant "good" reviews and rapid promotions. One Merrill Lynch managing director stated, "There's a bit of gluttony about wanting feedback. The millennial-narcissists were raised with so much affirmation and positive reinforcement that they come into the work place needing more."

Millennial-narcissists expect to be praised every day. Brought up to believe that living up to standards destroys one's self-respect or "sense of omnipotence," they are thin-skinned, entitled whiners unable to deal with criticism. An Ohio State University study revealed that such "narcissist leaders tend to have volatile and risky decision-making performance and can be ineffective and potentially destructive leaders."

Tough hard working "old school" investment bankers, who are known for their brutal sarcasm, particularly in down financial markets, have been compelled by human resource personnel to attend "praise" consultant lectures that instruct how to handle the fragile-egos of the young narcissists. Criticism is out, they are told; praise, for even completing the smallest of tasks, is in.

Then there are the smothering "Helicopter" parents who harass employers. These shameless, overly-protective, doting moms and dads think nothing about calling their child's boss and complaining about unsatisfactory reviews, disciplinary actions or perceived inadequate pay raises.

The 2008-2009 Great Recession has had a major impact on the lives of the millennium-narcissists and may have a humbling effect. The ones who were underperforming and constantly complaining were the first ones booted out the door of struggling companies – particularly on Wall Street. "The flights of narcissistic fantasy," Dr. Twenge reports, "were crashing to earth as risky mortgages failed and the money stopped flowing. The bursting of the credit bubble might suck the oxygen out of the system that narcissism needs to survive . . . it could slow its growth for several years."

Narcissist Elites and America's Body Politic

The "me generation" and millennium-narcissists have exhibited a craving for political power. Many believe they are the only ones fit to govern, not because they are lovers of the downtrodden or have experience, but because they are measurably smarter than the public at large and that society will benefit from their counsel.

The fact that these "aristocrats of talent" live insular lives, compound their prejudices by talking only to like-minded narcissists and have no idea as to the opinions or needs of

America's common folks, does not hinder their belief that they should be the nation's permanent ruling class. The social analyst, David Lebedoff, described these power-hungry narcissists this way:

> All their lives they have been told that they were superior to the rest of the populace – superior in intellectual ability as measured by certain tests. For them, that is enough. The most important tasks are awarded to those with the highest scores. This is essentially their view of government and it helps explain why the New Elite has so few precise views on the issues. For a group whose favorite political claim is to being completely "issue oriented," it is astonishingly devoid of any platform or agenda directed toward solving specific problems. When asked to produce one, its members invariably cite the problems, not the answers. A New Elitist "explains" his program by saying he is concerned with the economy and health care and the environment and so on. He is simply identifying the problems.

Narcissist elites have contempt for the democratic person and despise the political process because unenlightened, ordinary people might reject at the ballot box their self-proclaimed right to rule and their slogan-driven politics. To circumvent majority rule, particularly when it doesn't go their way, they pound the table and claim they are "morally superior," which is their way of saying they are smarter so they are always right. And anyone who doesn't agree is immoral. "The use of the word 'immoral'," Lebedoff observed, "is not intended to win arguments but to preclude them." And since being morally right is superior to the misguided majority, they hold that they have inherent right to be the managers of society, a class of managerial experts.

The concept of an elitist managerial class is not new. In 1941, New York University philosopher James Burnham published a prophetic book, *The Managerial Revolution: What Is Hap-*

pening in the World, to critical acclaim. *Fortune* called it the most debated book of the year. *Time* had it on its annual most notable list. And it made *The New York Times* best sellers. It was translated into a dozen languages.

Burnham (1905–1987), an ex-Trotsykyite who became a founding editor of *National Review*, held that self-destructing capitalism would not be replaced by socialism, which he thought "a mythical dream," but by a managerial class with an ethos all its own that administers policies. He agreed with Ludwig von Mises who wrote, "There is no sphere of human activity that they would not be prepared to subordinate to regimentation by the authorities. In their eyes, state control is the panacea for all ills."

In times of economic crisis, Burnham argued, the capitalist class – bankers, industrialists, merchants – will gradually be replaced by a new class of self-confident government managers. These administrative experts, directing engineers, and technocrats, will control ever-expanding government bureaus, agencies, and commissions that dictate how resources will be distributed. They will stress the state over individuals, will talk about planning more than free initiative, jobs over opportunity, and as "economic conditions progressively decay, the reward allocated to the finance-capitalists [will] seem inordinate and unjustified. . . ."

The managerial society will be promoted as the salvation of mankind ushering "in an age of plenty, sweetness, and light such that no man in his senses could do anything but welcome with rapture the prospect of the future." This is now a familiar note in both domestic and international politics, but somehow the illusion raises few eyebrows.

Reflecting on the Depression era, Burnham concluded that the psychological effect of the New Deal had been "to undermine public confidence in capitalist ideas and rights and institutions" and "to prepare the minds of the masses for the acceptance of the managerial social structure."

The Roosevelt administration created scores of federal

agencies that governed by fiat. The National Recovery Administration (NRA), for instance, determined prices and wages
throughout America until it was declared unconstitutional by
the U.S. Supreme Court. Subscribing to a "high wage" theory
that assumed efficient cost-cutting measures were bad, NRA
managers created volumes of price codes; every business, big
or small, had to comply. Policing the nation for violators, NRA
agents actually jailed a Cleveland couple who owned a dry
cleaner "because they cleaned suits for five cents less than the
NRA codes provides." Reviewing this managerial nightmare,
the world's leading liberal economist at the time, John May-
nard Keynes, dryly conceded that the NRA "probably impedes
recovery."

Franklin Roosevelt's rhetoric reflected managerial ideology. During the 1940 presidential campaign, Burnham found
that FDR's speeches "called for the support of all classes, including 'production men', 'technicians in industry' and 'managers' with one most notable exception: never by any of the
usual American terms of 'businessmen', or 'owners' or
'bankers' or even 'industry', did he address himself to the cap-
italists."

In the 1960s, President John F. Kennedy boasted that his administration hired managers who were the "best and the
brightest." In his seminal book of that title, David Halberstam
wrote, "if those years had any central theme, if there was anything that bound the [Kennedy] men, their followers and
subordinates together, it was the belief that sheer intelligence
and rationality could answer and solve anything."

The one appointment that epitomized this approach to governing was that of Robert Strange McNamara, a Harvard MBA,
who served as Secretary of Defense from 1961–1968. During
World War II he left his Alma Mater where he taught accounting, to become a data analyst in the Air Force Office of Statistical Control. It was in this job that McNamara became
convinced that most any problem could be solved by using reason supported by statistics. After the war he became Henry

Ford's "fastest wiz kid" and in 1960 he was the first non-family member to be elected president of the motor company. However, one week into that job, President-elect John F. Kennedy convinced McNamara to join his administration as Secretary of Defense.

McNamara, Halberstam has written, was the perfect Kennedy man because he "symbolized the ideal that [the New Frontier] could manage and control events in an intelligent rational way. Taking on a guerilla war was like buying a sick foreign company; you brought your systems to it." McNamara was to be Kennedy's number one "can-do-man" who Washington elites could trust to be always correct – even in choice of wars.

McNamara, whose favorite word was "quantification," was described by one colleague as possessing a mind that was "a beautiful instrument free from leanings and adhesions, calm and analytical." Senator Barry Goldwater called him, "an IBM machine with legs."

McNamara was a classic managerial narcissist. His biographer, Debora Shapley described him as an aloof and cold man who subscribed to an "ideology of impersonality" and "distained those he found average." One colleague said "[McNamara] loves humanity more than he loves human beings." He despised members of Congress because they dared to challenge his policies. Air Force Chief of Staff General Curtis LeMay characterized McNamara and his "Whiz Kids" this way:

> [They were] the most egotistical people that I ever saw in my life. They had no faith in the military; they had no respect for the military at all. They felt that the Harvard Business School method of solving problems would solve any problem in the world. . . . They were better than all the rest of us; otherwise they wouldn't have gotten their superior education, as they saw it.

For McNamara, quantitative planning drove everything. He was a behaviorist who was intellectually certain that armed with the proper data, one could develop five-year plans based on systems analysis and solve all of society's ills.

Like most narcissists, McNamara knew better than anyone else in the room because he was the ultimate rationalist. And, according to one McNamara friend, if you disagreed at a meeting, "you were not just wrong, you had violated something far greater, you had violated his sense of the rational order, like offending a man's religion." It was this intellectual hubris that led him to believe that war was nothing more than an engineering problem that could be won by applying analytical formulas and using slide rulers.

Vietnam War (a/k/a "McNamara's War") was a military disaster because strategic decisions were made not by frontline battlefield commanders, but by number crunching "quants" in the Pentagon who used metrics to determine bombing sorties. So-called proven business methods were applied to this war. McNamara's rationalist "Statistical strategy" methods did not lead to victory because the enemy was irrational, that is, the North Vietnamese and Vietcong were driven by ideological zeal and patriot fervor, not quantitative data. Even when McNamara decided the war could no longer be won, he based it on his analysis that the war was no longer cost effective. Bombing the north, he reported, cost ten dollars to get one dollar of damage.

Despite the disaster in Vietnam, the managerial class was not discredited and has continued to expand in the last third of the twentieth century. Today there are more than 400 Federal agencies, programs and activities that include the Administration for Children, Youth and Families (ACYF), Animal and Plant Health Inspection Service (APHIS), Community Relations Service (CRS), Economic Regulatory Administration (ERA), Office of Human Development Services (HDS), Labor-Management Services Administration (LMSA), New Community Development Corporation (NCDC), Office of Community Services (OCS), Public Health Service (PHS), Rehabilitation Services Administration (RSA), Senior Community Service

Employment Program (SCSEP), Urban Development Action Grant (UDAG), Volunteer Management Support Program (VMSP), Work Incentive Program (WIN), and Young Volunteers in Action (YUA). If you think that's a mouthful, wait until you see the coming growth of these alphabet agencies.

In the Age of Barack Obama, the economic crisis opened whole new vistas to managerial types. *New York Times* columnist David Brooks claims the new standards are being dictated by what he calls "Ward Three morality." Ward Three is a neighborhood in northwest Washington, D.C., populated by regulators, staffers, lawyers and senior civil servants – the new managerial class. According to Brooks, this crowd, even though they are powerful and feared at their workplaces, are resentful because their incomes do not match their sense of their own importance and cannot finance the lifestyle they believe they deserve. As a result, writes Brooks, "People in Ward Three have nationalized extravagance and privatized Puritanism."

The agenda of Obama's professional governing class is not limited to economics. Obama Czars and regulators are reaching into every home and church. Their significance in the world hinges on the transformation of America into a Ward Three nation. For them, liberty means obedience to the enlightened values of a managerial elite.

I, Obama: Narcissist-in-Chief

During the period of Republican ascendency (1968–2004), America's alienated intellectual narcissists hid in the weeds anxiously waiting for a political savior who would turn out the ill-informed fascist rascals and impose a new social order based on their rigid ideological formulas which they were certain would bring about equality and prosperity. Bitter and angry that they did not have the power they believed they were entitled, these narcissists were contemptuous of most Americans who went to the ballot box, particularly blue-collar voters who were not inclined to follow their lead. In their judgment, these shallow people were not properly cultivated and did not have the proper education or the correct values to make sound political and public policy choices. To deal with these sorely wanting masses, they preached an illiberal egalitarianism. These zealots, particularly radical environmentalists, feminists and social justice advocates, were intolerant authoritarians who historian Richard Hofstadter described as reformers who embrace "hatred as a form of creed."

During their political wilderness years, narcissistic warriors created an incredible paper trail detailing their anti-democratic tendencies. Here's a sampling:

First Earthers have called on American's to "shake off this awful thing called Western culture which has now, inevitably, brought the world to the brink of ecocide." To save the world, one leading environmentalist, William Ophuls, called for "a government possessing great powers to regulate individual behavior in the common interest." He demanded "the loss of rights we now possess." Ophuls' confreres have proclaimed that in their "war to save the planet" their fight "is the holiest fight of all!" and they demand an "Eco-Jihad."

One leading environmentalist, Dave Foreman, who broke with the Earth First! movement because of their authoritarian tendencies, made these observations about the dangers of this revolutionary Vanguard in *Earth First! Journal*:

> When we create such a world, our opponents become the enemy, become the *other*. . . . In such a dichotomous world, they lose their humanness and we lose any compulsion to behave ethically or with consideration toward them. In such a psychological state, we become true believers and any action against the enemy is justified. One needs only to look at Adolf Hitler or the Ayatollah Khomeini to see the results to one's psyche of holding this attitude.

Another group of authoritarian narcissists are radical feminists. In his work, the *Dark Side of the Left*, Professor Richard Ellis points out that these extremists held that most women "suffered from false consciousness" and not only despised those considered responsible for their plight (i.e., men) but also have a condescending and smug attitude towards all women who dare to disagree with their platform. "Radical feminist groups such as Cell 16," Ellis reports, "insisted that those women who wanted children merely showed they had 'not achieved sufficient maturity and autonomy.'"

"The Feminists," founded by Ti-Grace Atkinson, is another example of a feminist organization that restricts membership based on their ideological narcissism. Because they hold that marriage is an "inherently inequitable institution" and that rejecting it is "both in theory and in practice [is] a primary mark of the radical feminist," the By-Laws state that only one third of its members can be married or living with men.

In the field of social-justice education, the leading narcissist warrior has been Bill Ayers, co-founder of the terrorist Weatherman group. The Weatherman, who called for the violent over-throwing of the "evil capitalist" U.S. government, were responsible for numerous building bombings and criminal activities all over the nation. In 1970, a Weatherman pipe bomb explosion killed one San Francisco policeman and wounded another. While making nail bombs intended for Fort Dix military base in New Jersey, Weatherman plotters blew themselves up. Three were killed and a Greenwich Village brownstone, which housed their bomb manufacturing plant, was completely destroyed. When attempting to rob a Brink's armored truck in Nanuet, New York in 1981, underground Weatherman murdered two policemen and a security guard.

Ayers, whose federal riot and bombing indictment was dropped in 1974 due to illegal wiretaps, never showed remorse for Weatherman domestic terrorist activities and his involvement in setting off explosions in the Pentagon and U.S. Capitol, wrote in his 2001 memoir *Fugitive Days*, "I don't regret setting bombs. I feel we didn't do enough." The Weatherman, he concluded, "showed remarkable restraint."

In his forties, after receiving a Ph.D. in education from Columbia University in 1987, Ayers began a new career as a professor at the University of Illinois at Chicago and as trainer of teachers for the Chicago school system.

Ayers has been promoting "social justice" education methods which, according to *Education Week*, recommends critical pedagogy – "teaching kids to question whoever happens to hold the reins of power at a particular moment. It's see yourself not just as a consumer, but as an actor-critic." Students are to be taught to recognize that America is nothing more than a racist, sexist, oppressive capitalist nation.

The University of Illinois catalog description of the course Ayers taught for years, "On Urban Education," reads like a Marxist pamphlet: "Homelessness, crime, racism, oppression – we have the resources and knowledge to fight and overcome these things. We need to look beyond our isolated situations to define our problems globally. We cannot be child advocates . . . in Chicago or New York and ignore the web that links us with the children of India or Palestine."

These narcissist-warriors who believed every problem or injustice could be solved by like-minded government bureaucrats dictating to the masses, believed their time had arrived in 2000. The Democratic nominee for president, Al Gore – a classic narcissist child of privilege who believed he was bred to be president and took credit for most everything including the invention of the Internet – was their dream candidate. And when the U.S. Supreme Court in effect awarded the closely-contested election to George W. Bush, these warriors went off the deep end. Many denounced the system as hopelessly corrupt and argued that the Republicans had conspired to steal the election. Some went so far as claim an *X-Files* fascist plot – Votomatic software was programmed to discount every tenth Gore vote.

Four years later these same elites were enraged that voters rejected another of their anointed ones, Senator John Kerry of Massachusetts. They portrayed President Bush as a "thug" and "killer" in league with Bin Laden, accused him of Nazi-like policies, warned that rape would be legal if he were re-elected; and said that like the half-witted Fredo in *The Godfather*, should be shot.

Shocked that Election Day surveys revealed voters were in sync with Bush's moral values and considered it the top issue, the elitist intellectuals came out swinging. In *The New York Times*, Garry Wills wrote on the November 4 op-ed page that "many more Americans believe in the Virgin Birth than in Darwin's theory of evolution." The *Times'* Maureen Dowd accused Republicans of dividing America "along fault lines of fear, intolerance, ignorance and religious rule." E.J. Dionne of *The Washington Post* blamed Kerry's defeat on "the exploitation of strong religious feelings." Ronald Dworkin wrote in the *New York Review of Books* that Bush's alliance with the religious Right has already "proved a serious threat to America's commitment to social inclusiveness."

Thomas Frank, author of *What's the Matter with Kansas*, looked upon the GOP "vote your values" strategy as a corporate Wall Street cover up: "The culture wars, in other words, are a way of framing the ever-powerful subject of social class. They are a way for Republicans to speak on behalf of the forgotten man without causing any problems for their core big-business constituency."

The Democratic Party's narcissist elites, however, felt no blame for the loss. It was inconceivable to them that their views were out of the mainstream. Columnist George Will summed up the distain these Democrats had for the judgment of the majority of Americans:

A small but significant, because articulate, sliver of the Democratic Party seems to relish interpreting the party's defeat as validation. This preening faction reasons as follows: the re-election of George W. Bush proves that 51 percent of the electorate are homophobic, gun-obsessed, economically suicidal, anti-science, theocratic dunces.

Therefore to be rejected by them is to have one's intellectual and moral superiority affirmed.

In 2008, to finally get their hands on the levers of power,
the enlightened class decided to support for president one of
their own, Barack Hussein Obama.

Obama is the model intellectual/political narcissist. He attended the correct undergraduate school, Columbia University.
While living in New York City, Obama participated in Socialist
Scholar Conferences and worked briefly for Ralph Nader's leftist organization, New York Public Interest Research Group
(NYPIRG). Having decided he wanted to become a community
organizer, he moved in 1983 to the nation's hotbed for that pro-
fession – Chicago.

Unable to give a concise description of the duties of Community Organizing to friends, he lectured them on the need for
change. "Change in the White House, where Reagan and his
minions were carrying on their dirty deeds. Change in the Congress, compliant and corrupt. . . . Change won't come from the
top, I would say. Change will come from a mobilized grass
roots."

As a candidate for president in 2008, Obama was very defensive about his time as a community organizer – particularly
when Governor Sarah Palin and other Republicans publicly
mocked him as having been nothing more than a big-talker
with no real responsibility. The Obama campaign's rhetorical
smokescreen – "Jesus was an organizer, Pontius Pilate was a
governor," was understandable because community organizing has had a checkered history.

The original intent of the "War on Poverty" was to encourage "maximum feasible participation" of inner city residents
in their quest for community. However, social diagnosticians,
whose goal was to create a permanent poverty industry,
changed the language in the Economic Opportunity Act of 1964
to read that there be "maximum feasible participation of public
agencies and non-profits" in poor neighborhoods.

That simple clause was responsible for the rise of

community organizers who Daniel Patrick Moynihan described as "guerillas living off the administrative countryside" exercising power without the corresponding responsibility. Unlike neighborhood pols who were accountable to the electorate, they did not have to fear punishment for wrong or unpopular actions.

These anti-poverty warriors subscribed to radical Saul Alinsky's principles that one must organize to "rub raw the sores of discontent" and that conflict is the basis of community organization.

In this spirit, a 1969 draft of the Office of Economic Opportunity's Trainer's Manual for Community Action Agency Heads actually encouraged "threat power" as an appropriate tool for community organizers:

> *Threat power* – the ultimate threat power is the riot. This is clearly against the public law, the national standards of conduct and the rules of OEO; and it is most destructive to the citizens most in need. But it is important that Board members recognize the *threat power* of rioting as a very real power and possibility.

Hundreds of millions of dollars that poured into community action programs were dedicated to supporting professional rabble-rousers, not the downtrodden. New York City's Democratic mayor, Robert Wagner, complained to the White House in 1965, that community organizers were "becoming full-time paid agitators and organizers for extremist groups." One old time lefty, Stanley Aronowitz, Chairman of Manhattan's West Side Committee for Independent Political Action, conceded that the only benefit of the Great Society's largesse was "it has given employment to the organizers."

After studying the community organizing programs of the sixties, Moynihan concluded they consisted of soaring rhetoric, minimum performance, feigned constancy, private betrayal. There was not "maximum feasible participation" but "maximum feasible misunderstanding."

Despite dismal results, to this day thousands of community organizing groups continue to be funded by taxpayer dollars and tax-exempt foundations to promote leftist ideological agendas.

As the Chicago Director of the Development Communities Project, Stanley Kurtz reports in his work *Radical-in-Chief*, Obama "lived and worked – by conviction – in the midst of Chicago's largely hidden socialist world." He was also an instructor at the Gamaliel Foundation teaching future organizers Saul Alinsky's *Rules for Radicals* that emphasized the changing rules of power (a/k/a destroying capitalism and embracing socialism).

In the fall of 1988, at age 27, Obama gave up his organizing jobs and entered Harvard Law School. He went on to become president of the *Law Review* (he never penned an article for the *Review*) and worked as a summer associate in the Chicago firms Sidley-Austin and Hopkins & Sutter. After graduating magnum cum laude in 1991, Obama turned down jobs with prestigious real law firms that would have required long hours and years of hard work to achieve a partnership and monetary success. Instead he accepted a fellowship at the University of Chicago in order to write a book on voting rights. Although he accepted a publisher's advance, that book was never written. However, he did present to the publisher a manuscript about himself. *Dreams from My Father* was the first of two personal memoirs he would write in his thirties.

Obama went on to serve from 1992 to 1996 at the University of Chicago Law School as lecturer and senior lecturer on Constitutional Law and as an associate and counsel for a small law firm specializing in civil rights litigation (1993–2004). Oddly, his law license became inactive in 2002.

During this period, Obama continued to be a community activist. He was Director of Illinois Project Vote (1992) and served on the board of the Woods Foundation (1993–2002) which funded scores of leftist Chicago organizations and causes.

To seek elective office, he was also developing a cadre of political contacts, including Rev. Jeremiah Wright, Bill Ayers, Bernadine Dohrn and Rev. Michael P. Pfleger. Contrary to Obama's later claims that Ayers was just "a guy in the neighborhood" whose alleged crimes were committed when Obama was only 8 years old, Obama had a close relationship with the unrepentant Sixties terrorist.

In a published article, Obama had written that he admired Ayers' social justice educational work. They served on the Woods Foundation board together and Ayers helped Obama become Chairman of the Chicago Annenberg Challenge which funded many of Ayers' pet radical projects. Obama also launched his candidacy for state senator in 1996 at a fundraiser held in Ayers' living room.

State Senator Obama – who represented Chicago's South Side and Hyde Park (1997–2004) before being elected U.S. Senator in 2004 – employed Saul Alinsky's techniques of concealing his extreme left-wing ideology. He portrayed himself as a moderate, bi-partisan, pragmatic technocrat who side-stepped controversy by voting "present" on legislation over 200 times.

Throughout Obama's Chicago years he not only laid the groundwork to start a career in elective office, he made career decisions that reflected his narcissist personality. As Charles Krauthammer put it, Obama's "talents have been largely devoted to crafting and chronicling his own life."

Community organizers and law professors do not exactly exhaust themselves – and Obama was not an exception. He never had to make tough executive decisions, didn't have to meet a payroll or make deadlines. He never had to sit behind a desk all day getting through mounds of paperwork and he never had to look people in the eyes and fire them.

Obama spent most of his time talking to like-minded people and sycophants in his radical-chic Hyde Park neighborhood reinforcing the belief that he was one of the anointed ones destined to lead a nation of dopes. One major league

Chicagoan who dealt with State Senator and U.S. Senator Obama told me that in a typical one-hour meeting, Obama would talk for 55 minutes then conclude by saying "I guess we both agree." When he was told that was not the case, Obama would take offense and abruptly end the meeting.

Obama was bored being a member of the Illinois legislature and the U.S. Senate because he was only one of many, not the center attraction. Also moving legislation requires hard work, attention to detail and massaging the egos of fellow legislators – not exactly Obama strengths.

Running for the Democratic nomination for president was tough for Obama. Candidates require not only fire in the belly, iron-will, thick skin, incredible stamina and the common touch with voters from all walks of life. Obama, accustomed to Hyde Park groupies hanging on to his every word, had serious trouble relating to Americans who held hum-drum jobs and main street values.

Barack Obama's long shot campaign strategy was to win caucus-states utilizing Saul Alinsky community-organizing techniques to rally targeted turnout. Many analysts believed that if this approach produced a few victories or good showings, Obama might secure the vice presidential nomination or position himself as a 2012 front-runner. But when Hillary Clinton's strategy to lock up the nomination early in the primary season backfired, Obama suddenly became a serious contender who had to take her on in the big primary states.

Competing in the delegate-rich rust-belt states was a challenge for Obama. The man who the *National Journal* rated in 2008 as the most liberal member of the Senate, had to morph into a moderate. To this end, he employed the Alinskyite stealth doctrine, a classic end-justifies-the-means approach: do whatever it takes to obscure one's real agenda if that agenda is too radical for the electorate. In Obama's case, the candidate was a reformer, an advocate of "hope and change," rather than a proponent of bigger government, higher taxes, more spending and more regulations.

The long primary season was almost too much for Obama. He constantly complained that schedules were exhausting, there were too many events, not enough time for sleep or relaxation. He was always late for prep sessions and would frequently cut them short. Obama, whose previous workdays centered around fashionable cocktail parties, couldn't hack grueling 20-hour days of retail politics.

Campaigning in Ohio, Pennsylvania, and Indiana, he was unable to relate to core voters in these states – blue collar working-class Americans. One pundit described it as the "Arugula Gap." Beer and burger voters did not react well when Obama asked, "anybody gone into Whole Foods lately and seen what they charge for arugula?" Expensive organic foods and trendy specialty foods may be the everyday fare of Hyde Park elitists but not for unemployed manufacturing workers who shop at Wal-Mart. In these old industrial states, Obama lost because he could not overcome the impression that he was an unemotional, condescending, detached, arrogant, remote academic type who did not understand the daily concerns of most Americans. He lost because he could not expand his appeal beyond fellow narcissists: college professors, graduate students and upper-income professionals.

Obama revealed over and over again that he had an elitist tin ear. When it became public that his long-time pastor and close friend, Jeremiah Wright, of Trinity United Church of Christ, made scores of racist and anti-American statements – including one that described the 9/11 terrorist acts as "America's chickens . . . coming home to roost" – Obama was too politically dense to grasp the impact Wright's slurs would have on the electorate. His first response was to complain that Wright's statements were taken out of context. Then he changed his tune a bit telling *The Chicago Tribune* that Wright is "like your uncle who says things you profoundly disagree with, but he's still your uncle." To further defend Wright, Obama "threw under the bus" his white grandmother who brought him up; "I can no more disown [Wright] than I can my white grandmother . . . who once confessed her fear of black men who passed her by the street, and who on more than one occasion has uttered racial ethnic stereotypes that made me cringe."

Thanks to an adoring press, Obama got off easy during the Wright crisis. None of them really explored how Obama could have attended Wright sermons for 20 years and never found anything odd or wrong or downright ugly about his tirades. A frustrated Hillary Clinton, livid over the media's double standards, got it right when she said, "Just imagine just for fun, if my pastor from Arkansas said the kind of things his pastor said. I'm just saying. Just imagine. This race would be over."

Obama compounded his poor relationship with working-class Democrats when it was revealed that he often did not put his hand on his heart when the national anthem was sung and that he "wasn't inclined to wear an American flag lapel pin" in the post 9/11 era. His wife, Michelle, did not help his cause when she said at a Wisconsin rally, "for the first time in my adult lifetime, I'm proud of my country."

Two weeks before the April 2008 Pennsylvania primary, Obama was caught on tape describing his genuine feelings about America's common folks at a San Francisco fundraiser packed with that city's leading elitist Democrats. "You go into some of these small towns in Pennsylvania, and like a lot of small towns in the Midwest, the jobs have been gone now for twenty-five years and nothing's replaced them," Obama told the group. "So it's not surprising then that [people there] get bitter, they cling to guns or religion or antipathy to people who aren't like them or anti-immigrant sentiment or anti-trade sentiment as a way to explain their frustrations."

Clinton, who was downing whiskey shots and beer in Pennsylvania pubs to prove she was in sync with Rust Belt voter values struck back with lightning speed. "America needs a president that will stand up for them, not a president that looks down on them," she said.

In the final stretch of the 2008 race for the Democratic presidential nomination, Obama had a tough time being in the front-runner spotlight. When, during the Pennsylvania debate, ABC's Charles Gibson asked a serious question about the capital gains rate, Obama flubbed it and afterwards had his staff beat up Gibson and co-moderator George Stephanopoulos complaining they purposely asked mean questions.

Obama, who presented himself as a different, sincere, transparent statesman above the old politics of personal destruction would, when it suited his cause, resort to political tricks and smears. When Bill Clinton tried to dismiss the significance of Obama's South Carolina primary victory by comparing it to Jesse Jackson's similar victory in 1988, Obama followed the "play the race card" script his staff gave him: "Hold on a second," he said. "So former President Clinton dismissed my victory in South Carolina as being similar to Jesse Jackson, and he's suggesting that somehow I had something to do with it?...Ok, well, you better ask him what he meant by that."

Outraged by Obama's appeal to racial politics, the distinguished Princeton historian Sean Wilentz wrote in *The New Republic*, "To a large degree, the [Obama] campaign strategists turned the primary and caucus race to their advantage when they deliberately, falsely, and successfully portrayed Clinton and her campaign as unscrupulous race-baiters. . . . [These tactics were] the most outrageous deployment of racial politics since the Willie Horton ad campaign in 1988."

After Clinton conceded the nomination to Obama in May 2010, the presumed nominee choreographed a messianic image. He told Congressional Democrats, "This is the moment . . . that the world is waiting for . . . I have become a symbol of the possibility of America returning to our best traditions." *Wall Street Journal* columnist Bret Stephens wrote that Obama portrayed himself as "the embodiment of a biracial, transcultural identity. He was supposed to make the oceans recede and the planet heal, as a champion of environmental good sense."

When Obama delivered his acceptance speech on the final night of the Democratic convention, it was not given before the party faithful in the delegate hall surrounded by family and party elders. No, Obama stood alone surrounded by Greek columns in Denver's Invesco Field before 75,000 adoring fans. Obama appeared to be accepting a crown, not a nomination.

Shortly after the convention, Obama displayed on his speaker's podium, a personal "great" seal. The campaign motto, "Yes We Can" was printed in Latin, *Vero Possumus*. This act of egoism was even too much for his adoring press, and the Obama For America seal was quickly discarded.

In the summer of 2008, Obama, in an unprecedented move for a presidential nominee, traveled to eight countries in ten days. In Berlin before a huge crowd, he behaved as though he was the head of the one world government, calling himself a "citizen of the world."

Reacting to the trip, the campaign of Republican nominee John McCain ran a TV ad that ridiculed Obama as "the biggest celebrity in the world" and portrayed him as another Britney Spears or Paris Hilton. The message, wrote Mark Halperin in *Game Change*, was that Obama was "precious, self-infatuated, effete, hoity-toity – a celebrelitist."

The thin-skinned Obama, who was supposed to be the post-racial candidate, reacted badly and once again used the race card to silence criticism. The day the McCain ad went up, Obama, campaigning in Springfield, Missouri, said, "Nobody really thinks that Bush or McCain have a real answer for the challenges we face, so what they're going to try to do is make you scared of me. 'You know, he's not patriotic enough. He's got a funny name. You know, he doesn't look like all those other presidents on those dollar bills, you know. He's too risky.'"

Obama, the super egoist, could not handle criticism. At one point in the fall campaign, he commanded his followers to go after all detractors: "I want you to talk to them whether they are independent or whether they are Republican. I want you to argue with them and get in their face." On another occasion he said of opponents (quoting a line from Brian De Palma's *The Untouchables*), "If they bring a knife to the fight, we bring a gun."

The man who called for "hope over fear, unity of purpose over conflict and discord" could break the rules he championed and get away with it because the high-minded, elitist, mainline press – with its contempt for ordinary people – looked the other way. They viewed Obama as a fellow member of the enlightened class destined to impose their ideology on the masses. And like all narcissists they looked upon those who dared to disagree as dumb. *Time* magazine's Joe Klein, a leading member of the pro-Obama chattering class, best summed up the contempt he and his confreres have for those who oppose their chosen one's policies: ". . . Americans are flagrantly ill-informed . . . and, for those watching FOX news, misinformed. It is very difficult to have a democracy without citizens. It is impossible to be a citizen if you don't make an effort to understand the most basic activities of your government. It is very difficult to thrive in an increasingly competitive world of you're a nation of dodos."

Obama could not only rely on media glitterati to cover for him but also to savage anyone who was perceived as a threat to his claim on the White House. In the fall campaign of 2008, such a person was Sarah Palin.

When John McCain announced that the governor of Alaska, Sarah Palin, was his V.P. choice, the Obama camp went into a state of shock. They couldn't believe that a "hick" who was once a cheerleader and a graduate of a backwater college in Utah could be taken seriously on the national political stage. Obama could not bring himself to utter her name. He initially referred to her as "the Mayor," the elected position she held before becoming governor.

To protect Obama and to destroy Palin, the elitist, feminist members of the media discarded all the rules of civility and fair play. They turned to what liberal historian Richard Hofstadter referred to as the "paranoid style in American politics" which consists of "the qualities of heated exaggeration, suspiciousness, and conspiratorial fantasy."

These feminists called her a hayseed, a bimbo, a toned-down version of a porn actress, and mocked her faith and small-town roots. Here's a sampling of the malicious statements:

> "[Palin's nomination] is a political gimmick . . . I find it insulting to women, to the Republican party, and the country." – Sally Quinn, *Newsweek*

> "[Republicans] have a tradition of nominating fun bantam-weight cheerleaders from the West." – Maureen Dowd, *The New York Times*

> "What her Down syndrome baby and pregnant teenage daughter unequivocally prove, however, is that her most beloved child is the anti-abortion platform that ensures her own political ambitions with the conservative right." – Cintra Wilson, *Salon*

> "I found Palin's selection insulting." – Ruth Marcus, *The Washington Post*

> Governor Palin's nomination "is a slap in the face to all women." – Michelle Cottle, *The New Republic*

According to the leftist *Daily Kos* website, Palin's children were not "off-limits" because, "They are the direct result of the lunatic abstinence-only garbage and should be highlighted as such." And *The New Republic* didn't spare Trig, her Down syndrome baby: "Palin has pursued environmental policies that seem perfectly crafted to swell the ranks of special needs kids."

When these leftists ran out of vicious comments, they made things up. They falsely accused Palin of speaking in tongues, slashing funds for pregnancy centers and the mentally disabled, and claimed her daughter was the real mother of her Down syndrome child.

On election night, November 4, 2008, in Chicago's Grant Park, President-elect Obama acknowledged his victory. When he addressed the nation, he was not surrounded by family, key advisors or supporters – he stood alone. It was all about him – and only him. In fact, the entire campaign was about him. The man who said, "I think that I'm a better speechwriter than my speechwriter. I know more about policies on any particular issue than my policy directors. And I'll tell you right now that . . . I'm a better political director than my political director," was now the Narcissist-in-Chief.

As president, Obama discarded the veneer of moderation and implemented the most radical big government agenda in the nation's history. By nationalizing aspects of the financial, automobile and health-care industries, Obama expanded the managerial state far beyond the visions of Woodrow Wilson and Franklin Roosevelt. Obama is not a pragmatist but a statist: "The president," observes historian Victor Davis Hanson, "believes that a select group of affluent, highly educated technocrats . . . supported by a phalanx of whiz-kids fresh out of blue-chip universities with little or no experience in the market place, can direct our lives far better than we can ourselves."

To stifle congressional and public opposition to his far-left ideological plans, Obama appointed over two dozen fellow narcissists – "Czars" – with bureaucratic authority to design plans to enable the managerial state to engineer order and to impose Obama's social justice ideals. These "choice architects," wrote journalist Andrew Ferguson, were empowered to arrange "the everyday choices that members of the public face in such a way that they'll naturally do the right thing – eat well, conserve energy, save more, drive safely, floss."

The late Senator Robert Byrd's warning to the White House that the flock of Czars "threaten the Constitutional systems of checks and balances" fell on deaf ears. In fact, Obama persuaded Senate Democrats to mow down congressional oversight legislation. Reacting to this expansion of executive power, a *Washington Times* editorial concluded: "Mr. Obama seems to have basic problems with democracy. He doesn't like it when people disagree with him; he resists compromise, and he seems to think he should be free to reshape the country to suit his vision."

The man who was to be a uniter and the post-partisan president shut down an exchange of ideas with Republican leaders by announcing, "I won the election." When former opponent, Senator John McCain voiced a contrary opinion in a policy discussion, Obama dismissed him saying "John, the election is over," and reminded him that "Only I'm the president of the United States . . . and I'll carry out my responsibilities the way I think appropriate."

At one so-called bipartisan session when Senate Minority Leader Mitch McConnell told the president that speaking time was not fairly allocated, Obama replied, "You're right. There was an imbalance on the opening statement because – I'm the president . . . I didn't count my time in terms of dividing it equally." At another gathering when Tennessee Senator Lamar Alexander tried to ask a question during an Obama filibuster, Obama rudely cut him off saying, "Let me just finish Lamar." These sessions were not bipartisan exchanges of ideas, but presidential lectures and photo-ops. Political columnist, Jed Babbin, concluded the central aspect of Obama's bipartisanship scam is that Republicans must "let him set the terms of the debate and adopt his theory of government in order to be 'bipartisan.' To accept his terms, Obama demands that Republicans agree with his misstatements of fact."

People who disagreed with the Obama agenda were accused of "fear mongering." The White House demonized dissent going so far as to urge supporters to report people who dared to criticize Obamacare. White House media director told Obama disciples, "If you get an e-mail or something on the web about health insurance that sounds fishy, send it to flag@white-house.gov."

When members of the media were perceived as critical of Obama, his staff would not hesitate to demonize them. White House aide David Axelrod went so far as to assert that Fox News Channel is "not really a news station. It's not just their commentators but a lot of their news programming, it's really not news. It's pushing a point of view."

Obama's dismissive attitude toward the press was even too much for Maureen Dowd the very liberal *Times* columnist. Dowd, who had compared Obama to the "haughty, reserved and fastidious Mr. Darcy," in *Pride and Prejudice,* wrote in a June 2010 column:

> The former constitutional lawyer now in the White House understands that the press has a role in the democracy. But he is an elitist, too, as well as thin-skinned and controlling. So he ends up regarding scribes as intrusive, conveying a distaste for what he sees as the fundamental unseriousness of a press driven by blog-around-the-clock deadlines.
>
> The 21st-century press beast is a scary multimedia monster, caught up in the trite as well as the vital, and reporters rarely can be as contemplative as the cerebral Obama would like...
>
> But that's the world we live in. It hurts Obama to be a crybaby about it, and to blame the press and the "old Washington game" for his own communication failures.

The columnist Michael Goodwin wrote in August 2009 that Obama's "the rock star turned salesman and everything in his administration depends on his stage act." The personal pronouns "I," "My" and "Me" were President Obama's favorite words. Word counters have pointed out that in his first State of the Union speech he used the word "I" ninety-six times;

"my" and "me" eighteen times. Fox News had calculated that after nine months in office he had referred to himself 1,109 times in forty-one formal speeches.

But when it came time to explain political or policy set-backs, the "I" word was not heard. The fault always rested on the shoulders of the uniformed masses. Midway through the second year of his administration, he said in an ABC News interview:

> If there's one thing that I regret this year, [it] is that we were so busy just getting stuff done and dealing with the immediate crises that were in front of us, that I think we lost some of that sense of speaking directly to the American people about what their core values are and why we have to make sure those institutions are matching up with those values.

He didn't speak to the American people enough? Because he is incapable of spending long hours behind a desk dealing with details and making tough executive decisions, Obama spent more time out of the White House lecturing, speechmaking, vacationing and playing golf than any of his predecessors. In his book *Crimes Against Liberty*, David Limbaugh points out that in his first year in office, Obama made 411 speeches and sat for 158 interviews. "He held twenty-three town hall meetings, made forty-six out-of-town trips to fifty-eight cities and thirty states, made ten foreign trips to twenty-one nations, held twenty-eight political fundraisers and attended seven campaign rallies for three Democratic candidates (all of whom lost, further illustrating the counter productive effect of his tired rhetoric.)"

When the Democratic Party suffered the biggest loss for an in-power party in a president's first mid-term election since 1922, Obama claimed the fault was not in his policies but the failure to communicate them properly. He told the *National Journal* that promoting his agenda was "a lot for me to be able to communicate effectively to the public in any coherent way." And the other reason for 63 Democrats losing their congressional seats was an uninformed electorate. "Facts and science [do] not seem to be winning the day," he said, ". . . because we're hardwired not to always think clearly when we're scared."

Reviewing his first two years in office, David Limbaugh wrote this incisive description of Obama:

> Based on his behavior as president, it is clear he truly believes his own hype, for we have discovered that instead of messianic, Obama is acutely, perhaps clinically, narcissistic. He behaves and governs as though he has been sheltered all his life, or at least since he was a young adult, living in a bizarre bubble, hearing only positive reinforcement and made to believe in his own supernatural powers. This is a major reason he cannot bear opposition; this is a major reason he is not, in the end, a man of the people and deferential to their will, but a top-down autocrat determined to permanently change America and its place in the world despite intense resistance from the American people themselves.

The Narcissist-in-Chief and the other members of his generation who believe they are the "best and the brightest" have in common an inflated sense of themselves. For them the world is an extension of their intellect and emotions. Because they are the anointed ones, the people should be submissive to their exercise of power. Any who challenge their vision are unworthy, insensitive, evil, intellectually and morally bankrupt. These narcissist-warriors have no compunction to undercut the very foundations of our democracy and to impose the rule of a single elite.

But to their dismay the November 2010 election proved there are still a majority of Americans who are not prepared to accept the narcissist elites conceded belief in their own superiority and their ideological vision of how the nation should operate. They sent a strong message that the state under Obama has become too intrusive and too bossy. They rejected the notion that narcissist elites have a providential role and know what is best for America. Instead, they agreed with Christopher Lasch's belief that "democracy works best when men and women do things for themselves, with the help of their friends and neighbors, instead of depending on the state."

Chapter 2

Washington Narcissists

July 29, 2009

Obamacare: Will Seniors Have a Duty to Die?

The national health care debate has elicited President Obama's pledge that the proposed $1.3 trillion, 1,018-page government health insurance program is "not going to mess" with anyone's current coverage. But this does not ring true.

If Obamacare becomes law, expect Medicare – which represents 15 percent of the federal budget, consumes 11 percent of federal taxes, and has a future unfunded liability of at least $60 trillion (yes, trillion) – to be cut immediately.

According to Medicare expert Dr. Thomas Saving of Texas A&M, if the "federal income tax remains at the 50-year average of 10.89 percent of the nation's gross domestic product, the present value of all future federal income tax revenues from now to eternity is $99.3 trillion so that the Medicare debt of $61.6 trillion is 62 percent of all future federal tax receipts." Since the feds will not spend that much money to meet this financial obligation, its only alternative is rationing health care for the elderly.

President Obama began to lay the groundwork for "messing" with Medicare when he publicly mused that perhaps his grandmother (who died last fall) should not have had a hip replacement in old age.

Obama's top medical advisor, Dr. Ezekiel Emanuel (former Chief of Staff Rahm Emanuel's brother) has called for denying treatment to senior citizens outright. "Unlike allocation by sex or race," he recently wrote, "allocation by age is not invidious discrimination; every person lives through different life stages rather than being a single age. Even if twenty-five-year olds receive priority over sixty-five-year olds, everyone who is sixty-five years now was previously twenty-five years." This amounts to a clever tap dance for throwing the elderly over the side.

Dr. Emanuel holds that health care should be denied to those "who are irreversibly prevented from being or becoming participating citizens." In other words, his vision of health care reform assumes the government possesses the power to determine a citizen's worth. Medical procedures would not be determined by doctors who are sworn to do no harm but by bean-counting state and federal bureaucrats. Take my word for it: the exercise of such power will lead to government-sanctioned euthanasia programs.

Don't dismiss my prognostications as Orwellian fantasies – health care that rationalizes abandoning the elderly and infirm has been kicking around for a long time.

Back in 1920, medical professor Alfred Hoche and law professor Rudolf Binding, in their work *Release and Destruction of Lives Not Worth Living*, argued for "allowable killing" of the physically unfit. "The right to live," they claimed, "must be earned and justified not dogmatically assumed." They insisted that eliminating the physically unfit was purely "healing treatment" or "healing work."

Their pseudo medical and legal scholarship provided the justification for the Third Reich's unparalleled euthanasia programs that were responsible for the death of millions of innocent people.

At the Nuremberg trials, chief American counsel Robert H. Jackson viewed the progression of German euthanasia this way:

A freedom-loving people will find in the records of the war crimes trials instruction as to the roads which lead to such a regime and the subtle first steps that must be avoided. . . . To begin with, it involved only the incurably sick, insane and mentally deficient patients of the institution. . . . But "euthanasia" taught the art of killing and accustomed those who directed and those who administered the death injections to the taking of human life. . . . Once any scruples and inhibitions about killing were overcome and the custom was established, there followed naturally an indifference as to what lives were taken. . . . If one is convinced that a person should be put out of the way because, from no fault of his own, he has ceased to be a social asset, it is not hard to satisfy the conscience that those who are willful enemies of the prevailing social order have no better right to exist.

Today, the Netherlands – whose people were victims of the Nazis – deny medical treatment to patients every day. Dutch courts have ignored Justice Jackson's warning and have upheld even involuntary euthanasia or "termination of the patient without explicit request." A doctor need only ask himself "if he would accept life if he were in the patient's position" and if he knew (although not necessarily consulted) another doctor who would agree that under the given circumstances the patient's life is not worth preserving or is a "limited life." Traveling pools of doctors (known as the "Angels of Death" squads) are permitted to go out and employ euthanasia when a local physician or a family refuses the "treatment." Euthanasia is sometimes performed without the knowledge of treating physicians and some non-medical volunteers are allowed to give lethal injections. Twenty percent of the Netherlands' annual deaths are due to doctor intervention.

In the United States there are health care reform proponents who are driven to transform America according to their current view of its best interests, and the means for the changes they would effect is raw federal power. They deny the intrinsic value of man and seek total control over him – a crude utilitarianism that tries to calculate the greatest good for the greatest number. The state, not God, thus decides who lives or dies.

This culture of death crowd would have us abandon the sick and the elderly to "contain costs." Americans whose basic belief in the inalienable right to life have an obligation to oppose Obamacare and to promote a culture of compassion, one that ensures that every person lives – every moment of life until natural death – with dignity.

August 27, 2009

Obamascience

First President Obama appointed Dr. Ezekiel Emanuel, who supports limitations on end-of-life care, as his top medical advisor. Now he has named John Holdren, another culture-of-death stalwart, as his top science advisor.

This newest Obama czar openly stated his support for mandatory abortions in *Ecoscience: Population, Resources, Environment*, a book Holdren co-authored with Paul and Anne Ehrlich some years ago:

> There exists ample authority under which population growth could be regulated. It has been concluded that compulsory population-control laws, even including laws requiring compulsory abortion, could be sustained under the existing Constitution if the population crisis became sufficiently severe.

Ecoscience also casually mentions sterilants in drinking water or staple foods of those who "contribute to social deterioration," the implantation of long-term birth control devices in women who have already given birth to two or three children, and an *international* monitor empowered to enforce population limits on any nation under scrutiny. (The Ehrlichs and Holdren have claimed, quite implausibly, that they were just listing possibilities then under discussion.)

Grilled by Senator David Vitter about these and other disturbing views last month, Holdren stated that it was "no longer productive" to think about optimal population size – but conceded little else. The media, as has become their custom when some Obama appointee is revealed to have an outrageously radical past, merely noted the hysteria of Holdren's opponents but did not explore his positions.

The Obama administration's social planners stand in a long tradition of progressives who reject the Judeo-Christian belief in the sanctity of human life. Many people still doubt that liberal-minded people actually hold such beliefs, but, as history shows, American progressives have often endorsed eugenics and other morally repugnant practices. Eliminating *inferiors*, they argued, is permissible in the name of preserving society as a whole. Holdren and his allies wouldn't put it that way, because it plays badly – even to an adoring media. But they don't hesitate to talk about restraining population in the name of preventing climate change – one of Dr. Holdren's recent preoccupations.

And media acquiescence in progressive eugenics has its own long and "distinguished" past. E.L. Godkin, founder of the *Nation*, Herbert Croly, founder of the *New Republic*, and William Allen White, editor of the *Emporia* (Kansas) *Gazette*, endorsed population-control programs because, they believed, America should be governed and populated by its "superior classes."

In local politics, however, they faced formidable political machines dominated by Catholics, so progressives looked to Washington for national solutions. They demanded quota legislation to end immigration from eastern and southern Europe. A U.S. government-funded forty-two-volume Immigration Commission Report, presented to Congress in 1910 by Senator William Dillingham of Vermont, provided a pseudo-biological foundation for the restrictive immigration acts of 1921 and 1924.

Those Commission findings, described by historian Oscar Handlin as "neither impartial nor scientific," gave credence to anthropologist Madison Grant's belief that people from the Mediterranean basin, the Balkans, and Polish ghettos were vulgarizing America. Many distinguished Americans – Theodore Roosevelt included – endorsed the findings of the Dillingham report and its enabling legislation, which effectively cut off immigration of this "human flotsam."

By 1940, thirty states had enacted laws calling for compulsory sterilization of poor and mentally disabled citizens. The majority of these laws were based on the Model Eugenical

Sterilization Law, which called for the sterilization – "regardless of etiology or prognosis" – of criminals, mental patients, the feeble-minded, inebriates, the blind and the diseased, and included those with physical impairments (the deaf, the deformed, and the "dependent," which meant the homeless, orphans, and paupers).

Today's progressives prefer more vagueness in the categories for elimination: "unwanted pregnancies," fetuses with "birth defects," and, in developed countries especially, *any* children because of their large "carbon footprint." But the result for those never born is the same.

The strongest voice against all such schemes was and is the Catholic Church. In 1920 the *Catholic World* summed up the Church's position when it declared that she "uncompromisingly sets her face against all materialistic social experiments that outrage human dignity, go counter to elemental ethics . . . and lead to callous disregard of the weak elements of the community."

In his 1930 encyclical, *Casti Connubii*, Pope Pius XI wrote: "[W]here no crime has taken place and there is no cause present for grave punishment, [public magistrates] can never directly harm, or tamper with the integrity of the body, either for the reasons of eugenics, or for any other reason."

Prior to World War II, the eugenics movement was based on population genetics (i.e., that Anglo-Saxons are genetically superior to, say, the Irish). In our time, the movement is focused on individual genetics. French historian André Pichot explains the new approach this way: "Freedom of artificial selection [replaces] the dictatorship of natural selection. . . . The threat is to the individual not to the population; so likewise is the remedy."

At a conference about eugenics last month, Pope Benedict XVI warned that confidence in science "may not overshadow the primacy of ethics when human life is at stake."

John Holdren and many others who are joining the Obama administration are committed to state planning of reproductive and life-extending procedures, though they know it is impolitic to say so openly. If they are to be stopped, Catholics must once again uncompromisingly oppose this New Eugenics. If we don't, no one will be safe.

December 30, 2008

The Behaviorists Are Back

In his search for a prescription to cure America's ailing economy, President-elect Barack Obama is consulting scores of leftist interventionists including behavioral economists. *The New York Times* recently reported that Obama may hire economic psychologists "specifically charged with translating the lessons of the behavioral revolution into real-world policies." One proponent of this approach, Harvard economist Sendhil Mullainathan, told the *Times*, "The issues we struggle with today are inherently behavioral as never before. It's impossible to think of the current mortgage crisis without thinking seriously about underlying consumer psychology. And it's impossible to think of future regulatory fixes without thinking seriously about that issue." Excited by the prospects, the *Times* concluded, "The promise of behavioral economics is that it can help create a better government, one that wastes less money and does more to improve peoples' lives. That's hardly a modest goal."

It should come as no surprise that the 1970s radicals taking over the federal government in January are promoting this brand of economics because the hero of their youth was the leader of America's behavioral revolution, B.F. Skinner. Skinner, who, in the early 1970s made the cover of *Time* magazine and whose book *Beyond Freedom and Dignity* hit the *Times* bestseller list, proudly proclaimed to his adoring public, "We not only can control human behavior, we must!" Behaviorists like Skinner argue that psychology should be limited to observations and tenets related to behavior. As epistemological descendants of Descartes, they attempt to sever any connections between the study of man and philosophy, by methodologically denying the existence of the mind and the scientific validity of philosophical psychology in the Aristotelian and Thomistic sense.

Skinner and his followers deny the existence of the mind

and reduce human psychology to the mere study of intersub-jectively demonstrable events – that is, behavior. Consistent with Cartesian reductionism, qualitative differences are denied by behaviorists. By recognizing nothing beyond the perversely simple materialistic continuity derived from mere quantitative reductionism, behaviorists boast they can study rats to draw conclusions about man. Skinner emphasizes that man is no more responsible (nor laudable) for his creative accomplish-ments in music, art, literature, economics, science, and inven-tion, than is the warthog for his warts. Accordingly, there is then no essential difference between modern "objective" psy-chology and rodentology, or between man and rat.

Behaviorists also deny the freedom to choose between good and evil, the will to resist temptation or to succumb to sin. Skin-ner writes that man's struggle for freedom is not due to a will to be free but "to certain behavioral processes characteristic of the human organism, the chief of which is the avoidance or the escape from so-called aversive features of the environment." Moral choice, then, is nothing more than the tropism of an au-tomaton conditioned by various genetic, social, and historical contingencies.

The behaviorist wishes to control in his own image, every aspect of man in society. B.F. Skinner, in his novel *Walden II*, de-scribes this Utopia: "There is complete equality of the sexes in all things. Men and women marry and mate in their late teens, thus averting sexual frustration and its consequences. When the women are in their twenties, they have finished bearing all the children they want and they then take up personal goals. Babies are raised in communal nurseries, in which the mothers may work as they choose. The children grow up equally in an atmosphere of care and concern, free of envy, strife, shock, com-petition, and punishment."

Walden II's alleged perfect society is possible only through the application of a behavioral technique known as positive re-inforcement. The chief engineer and architect of the commu-nity, Frazier, exercises control in this fashion: "Now that we know how positive reinforcement works and why negative doesn't ... we can be more deliberate and hence more successful, in our cultural design. We can achieve a sort of control under which the controlled, though they are following a code much more scrupulously than was ever the case under the old system, nevertheless *feel free*. They are doing what they want to do, not what they are forced to do. That's the source of the tremendous power of positive reinforcement – there's no restraint and no revolt."

Skinner's society, based on behavioral methods, also takes the ideological position that democracy is not a worthy system of government: "The only solution is to make an honest admission that democracy is outmoded and replace it with a more effective system namely, technical meritocracy."

If behaviorists have their way, man will be dehumanized by the planning and redevelopment of the cultural, economic and social system by government overseers. What a scary intellectual basis for Washington's forthcoming managerial revolution.

Let's hope that the Obama administration turns out better than some of his more radical camp followers, because otherwise it's welcome to Barack's brave new world.

June 5, 2009

Margaret Sanger: Hillary's Hero

When Hillary Clinton was representing New York in the U.S. Senate, in order to placate her large Catholic and Jewish Orthodox and Hasidim constituencies, she called on Democrats to be more tolerant of the beliefs of those who oppose abortion. But now, reporting to the most pro-abortion president ever to hold that office, and not to the electorate, Secretary of State Clinton is revealing her genuine extremist positions on the subject.

At Planned Parenthood's recent annual gala in Houston, Mrs. Clinton, accepting its highest honor, the Margaret Sanger Award, said "I want to assure you that reproductive rights . . . will be a key to the foreign policy of this administration."

Let's see: North Korea is testing nukes and lobbing missiles, the Middle East is a tinderbox, Iran is developing a bomb, the economic crisis might destabilize international relations, but "reproductive rights" (a/k/a abortion) is a key issue in Hillary Clinton's State Department. The taking of innocent life gets the same priority as issues of war and peace. How absurd is that?

There's more: Secretary Clinton also told her adoring audience, "I admire Margaret Sanger enormously, her courage, her tenacity, her vision," and "Margaret Sanger's work is not yet done."

Let's be thankful her work is not yet done! Because Margaret Sanger (1879–1966) the founder of Planned Parenthood and the editor of *The Birth Control Review*, was one of America's leading proponents of a particularly crude kind of eugenics.

The belief that the evolution of the human race may be improved by programs of breeding which foster more desirable traits than nature alone may provide is called eugenics or *positive* eugenics. *Negative* eugenics (also known as dysgenics or cacogenics) would "purify" the gene pool by breeding out undesirable traits or by disposing of undesirable human beings: individuals, ethnic groups, or whole races.

Sanger embraced both approaches. "Eugenics," Sanger said in 1921, is "suggested by the most diverse minds as the most adequate and thorough avenue to the solution of racial, political, and social problems. The most intransigeant [sic] and daring teachers and scientists have lent their support to this great biological interpretation of the human race." Sanger boldly championed "more children for the fit, less from the unfit, that is the chief issue of birth control." And she believed she could provide the leadership necessary to identify undesirables and implement plans to intervene in their sex lives.

Born to Irish Catholic parents who raised eleven children, Margaret Sanger rejected Church teachings on procreation and proposed a *Code to Stop the Overproduction of Children Based on Common Sense Instead of Sentiment*, which asserted that no woman "has a legal right to bear children, and no man shall have the right to become a father without a permit for parenthood."

To restrict breeding, local government birth control clinics would be empowered to issue a limited number of birth permits to ensure that population growth would be controlled. Only those with proper genetic credentials and with the financial means to support a family would receive a permit for parenthood, valid for one birth. Those found biologically unfit, the "feeble-minded," would be sterilized. "There is only one reply to a request for a higher birth rate among the intelligent," Sanger wrote, "and that is to ask the government to *first* take the burden of the insane and feebleminded from your back. Sterilization for these is the solution."

Appalled by the influx of Southern and Eastern Europeans who landed on our shores in the early twentieth century, Sanger opened her first birth control clinic in Brownsville, Brooklyn, a neighborhood populated by what she considered "irresponsible breeders" – Slavs, Latinos, and Jews.

Sanger also condemned immigrant Italian Catholics for following Church teachings and propagating "feebleminded" children. According to Sanger, their population had degenerated to "very inferior racial health" due to the celibacy of intelligent Italian priests and nuns.

Sanger even found the democratic process wanting. In the April 1925 issue of *The Birth Control Review*, she opined: "We can all vote, even the mentally arrested. And so it is no surprise to find the moron's vote as good as the vote of the geniuses. The outlook is not a cheerful one." Claiming that elected representatives were "apparently mentally and constitutionally unfit," she called for qualifying intelligence tests for legislators.

"Progress," G.K. Chesterton observed, "has discouraged anybody who had anything to say in favor of man, in his common relations to manhood and motherhood and the normal appetites of nature. Progress has been merely the persecution of the Common Man." Margaret Sanger, one of America's most prominent progressives, devoted her life to trying to restrict Catholic and Jewish "human weeds," as she called them. Only an Anglo-Saxon "race of thoroughbreds," she preached, should be permitted to exist.

And now our nation's chief foreign policy spokesman calls on Sanger's heirs to finish her work. What a scary prospect for the world's common folks.

June 17, 2009

Sonia's Story

When the U.S. Supreme Court nominations of John Roberts and Samuel Alito were confirmed by the U.S. Senate in 2005, various groups and individuals were apoplectic that five Catholics sat on the nation's highest court. They complained that a judicial Catholic cabal might impose its religious views, overturn *Roe v. Wade,* and force millions of women back to America's dark alleyways to terminate unwanted pre-borns.

This year the liberal establishment does not appear to be upset over the nomination of another Catholic, Judge Sonia Sotomayor. That's because they view Sotomayor as merely a cultural Catholic, which to me means a Cafeteria Catholic – the familiar person who keeps the doctrines she likes and rejects those she finds inconvenient. Another reason her Catholicism doesn't matter to the usual opponents: in a recent interview with Senator Dianne Feinstein, she used the pro-*Roe v. Wade* code phrase – "I respect precedent."

Readers might recall during the Roberts confirmation hearings, Senator Charles Schumer asking if the nominee thought *Roe v. Wade* was a "super" precedent because it has been on the books for thirty plus years. Roberts wisely and without hesitation dismissed the inquiry, saying he had no idea what the Schumer-created term meant. Think about it. If one accepts Schumer's position, the 1896 Supreme Court decision *Plessy v. Ferguson,* which upheld a Louisiana "Jim Crow" law and established the "separate but equal" rule, should have been treated as a "super" precedent and upheld in *Brown v. Board of Education* (1954) and *Bolling v. Sharpe* (1954). Instead the court rightly overruled the fifty-six-year-old "separate but equal" doctrine, as it applied to schools.

Sotomayor's comments on identity – Latinas just have more wisdom – would be fatal for most potential justices, but have also been overlooked by President Obama and Senate Democrats. Here's a sampling:

- "I would hope that a wise Latina woman with the richness of her experience would more often than not reach a better conclusion than a white male who hasn't lived that life."
- "I simply do not know exactly what the difference will be in my judging. But I accept there will be some based on my gender and my Latina heritage."
- "I further accept that our experiences as women and people of color affect our decisions. The aspiration to impartiality is just that – it's an aspiration because it denies the fact that we are by our experiences making different choices than others."
- "I wonder whether by ignoring our differences as women or men of color we do a disservice both to the law and society."

Human persons, by their very nature, possess the power to reason as well as various non-rational impulses including passion, sentiment, prejudice, and intuition. Hence, it should not be a surprise that Sotomayor is passionate about her experiences as a Puerto Rican growing up in a poor Bronx neighborhood.

The New York City of Sotomayor's youth – as I can personally attest – was not a pleasant place to live. Great Society social engineering policies and programs were proving to be a prescription for bankruptcy and disorder. The ever growing problems of crime, drugs, finance, taxation, welfare, and education destroyed neighborhoods, created a permanent underclass, and brought the entire city to its knees.

Sotomayor's Bronx background and other life experiences, however, should not enter her decision-making any more than a white male's should. She will swear an oath of office which requires a judge's personal feelings to be subordinate to judicial duties. Before Sotomayor can sit with her eight colleagues she must swear to "administer justice without respect to persons, and do equal right to the poor and the rich and impartially discharge all the duties incumbent upon me as a U.S. Supreme Court Justice under the Constitution and laws of the United States." In other words, Sotomayor must administer justice as defined by the U.S. Constitution and its laws and not by her passions.

U.S. Circuit Court Judge James L. Buckley, a Catholic and brother of the late William F. Buckley, Jr., explained the duties of a federal judge this way: "The authority that was vested in me upon taking [the oath of office] is derived exclusively from the Constitution. Thus the justice I am sworn to administer is not justice as I might see it. . . . And if I consciously deviate from that body of law to do justice as I see it, I violate my oath of office and undermine the safeguards embodied in the Separation of Powers. Should I ever be asked to hear a case in which the application of the law might result in my material complicity in an immoral act, I would have to examine my conscience and, if it so dictated, recuse myself. What I may not do is bend the law to suit my conscience."

That's the proper definition of judicial temperament. And if Justice Sotomayor embraces it, her personal story will have little to do with her professional life.

July 14, 2009

Justice Ruth Bader Ginsburg: Eugenicist

In an interview published in last Sunday's *New York Times* magazine, U.S. Supreme Court Associate Justice Ruth Bader Ginsburg revealed the purpose for legalized abortion: "Frankly I had thought that at the time *Roe* [*v. Wade*] was decided, there was concern about population growth and particularly growth in **populations that we don't want to have too many of.**" (Emphasis added.)

What a deplorable statement. Unfortunately, the *Times* reporter failed to ask the obvious follow-up: What populations do we have too many of? Jews? African-Americans? Hispanic-Americans? Catholics? Fundamentalists? The poor? Welfare recipients?

This language about getting rid of "populations that we don't want to have too many of" – a/k/a undesirables or those "unfit to live" – is the standard endgame of a vile product of the social Darwinist movement: *eugenics*, the so-called science of good birth.

According to radical social Darwinists, people who are an economic or medical burden on society should be eliminated. To promote their agenda, they founded numerous organizations, including the Eugenics Record Office and the Cold Spring Harbor Eugenics Laboratory (funded by the Rockefellers, Harrimans, and Carnegies), and introduced eugenics legislation throughout the nation.

America's leading apostle of social Darwinism, William Graham Sumner of Yale (1840–1910), declared: "Let it be understood that we cannot go outside of this alternative: liberty, inequality, survival of the fittest; not liberty, equality, survival of the unfittest. The former carries society forward and favors all its best members; the latter carries society downwards and favors all its worst members."

Another eugenicist, Herbert Spencer (1820–1903), warned the developed nations not to foster the survival of the unfit by interfering with harsh economic realities. In the name of biology, he opposed free public education, sanitation laws, compulsory vaccinations, and welfare programs for those he called the "hereditary poor." He feared that these services would encourage the perpetuation of undesirable physical, intellectual, and social traits. Spencer's social Darwinism made the pseudoscience of eugenics "morally" permissible in the name of preserving "society as a whole."

Even Theodore Roosevelt caught eugenics fever. "Someday," wrote Roosevelt in 1913 to Charles Davenport, director of the Eugenics Record Office, "we must realize that the prime duty, the inescapable duty of the good citizen of the right type is to leave his or her blood behind him in the world, and that we have no business permitting the perpetuation of citizens of the wrong type."

In his work *Preface to Eugenics* (1940), Frederick Osborne of the American Museum of Natural History called for the segregation of the "hereditary defective" in state institutions: "It is doubtful whether democracy can long continue in any society except one whose operation favors the survival of competent people in every social and occupational group."

The National Socialists were the first to make eugenics a matter of public policy. The 1933 German racial legislation signed into law by Chancellor Hitler provided the legal foundation for the Nazi Final Solution of Europe's Jewish population and approved euthanasia, abortion, artificial insemination, electric-shock experiments, tissue and muscle experiments, fetal experimentation, and gas chambers. All these Nazi horrors took place in the name of eugenics. Joseph Goebbels ordered all German organizations to be educated in "the eugenics way of thinking!"

When the Nuremburg trials revealed the horrendous consequences of Nazi eugenics programs, the American movement went underground. The Cold Spring Harbor Eugenics Laboratory, for instance, dropped "Eugenics" from its title in an attempt to maintain respectability. Annals of Eugenics became Annals of Human Genetics. Eugenicists now called themselves "population scientists" or "human geneticists."

By the 1970s, however, the eugenics movement made a comeback with *Roe v. Wade*, their biggest victory. Reviewing this . . . *success*, journalist-philosopher Malcolm Muggeridge concluded, "For the Guinness Book of Records, you can submit this: that it takes about thirty years in our humane society to transform a war crime into an act of compassion."

The eugenics movement flourishes because public officials, like Justice Ginsburg, subscribe to an ideology that discards the sanctity of the human person. Believing that man is merely a machine or animal – not a person with a soul and, therefore, unique among God's creations – makes it easy for them to form a rational justification for getting rid of "populations that we don't want to have too many of."

It would be comforting to think that Justice Ginsburg will catch a lot of flack and be compelled to explain her outrageous comment in the *Times* to the American people. But this is one bit of news – and history – the *Times* is unlikely to think fit to print.

So let's at least remind ourselves of G.K. Chesterton's words back in 1915:

> [E]ugenics is chiefly a denial of the Declaration of Independence. It urges that so far from all men being born equal, numbers of them ought not to be born at all. And so far from their being entitled to life, liberty, and the pursuit of happiness, they are to be forbidden a form of liberty and happiness so private that the maddest inquisitor never dreamed of meddling with it before.

February 1, 2009

Inside the Beltway Ethics: Two Sets of Rules

Throughout the 2008 election campaign, Barack Obama pledged that his administration would give birth to a "new era of responsibility." Lobbyists and the ethically challenged would be banned from working in the executive branch. He would initiate "the most sweeping ethics reforms in history."

Despite Obama's lofty rhetoric, to date over a dozen lobbyists have received job waivers and tax-law violations of nominees have been overlooked. Columnist Michael Goodwin observed that Obama is "making Swiss cheese out of his executive order barring lobbyists from his administration." He concluded, "Instead of enforcing the ban he's busy poking holes in it."

Why are Democrats absolved for their ethical transgressions and Republicans punished? Because there are two sets of rules.

To prove my contention, let's review a few high-profile cases starting with Republicans:

- In 1985, Idaho Congressman George Hansen was indicted, convicted and served time in prison for failing to disclose to the House of Representatives loans made to him by Nelson Bunker Hunt.
- President Reagan's first national security adviser, Richard Allen, was hounded out of office by the media over three inexpensive watches he received from longtime friend Professor Tamotsu Takase.
- In January 1989, former U.S. Senator John Tower was the first cabinet nominee of a *new* president to be turned down by the Senate. Tower, a divorced man, was rejected as Secretary of Defense by his former colleagues because of rumors he was a womanizer.
- Senator Robert Packwood of Oregon resigned his seat in September 1995 after the Senate Ethics Committee recommended expulsion for sexual harassment.

Now the Democrats:

- Congressman Geraldine Ferraro (the 1984 Democrat V.P. candidate) received a pass for failing to reveal on Congressional disclosure forms that she owned stock in her husband's real estate corporation. It was considered a "mere oversight."
- Congressman and House Ways and Means Committee Chairman Charles Rangel, who failed to pay taxes on income from his Caribbean rental properties and whose disclosure forms have had a minimum of twenty-eight omissions in thirty years, was instantly forgiven by the members of his party for "minor mistakes."
- Charges of sexual harassment against President Clinton and the Lewinsky affair were dismissed by his party's leaders as politically motivated and an invasion of his private life.
- Connecticut Senator Chris Dodd, chairman of the Senate Banking Committee, got an ethics pass for receiving preferential mortgage rate treatment from the scandal-ridden and now defunct Countrywide Financial.
- Although Tim Geithner admitted he owed more than $48,000 in back taxes, his nomination as Treasury secretary and overseer of the IRS was never in doubt because his supporters believed it was an "honest error."
- Despite revelations that former Senator Tom Daschle owed more than $120,000 in back taxes and made millions at a Washington law and lobbying firm – even though he is neither a lawyer nor a registered lobbyist – his nomination for Secretary of Health and Human Services was not in serious trouble. Senate Democrats concluded his public apology was sufficient penance and President Obama said he "absolutely stood" behind his nominee. After Daschle's withdrawal, the White House announced the president did not force him to do so and accepted his decision with "sadness and regret."

Notice the double standards?

It all comes down to one's definition of "ethics." For me, ethics means something like the classical conception: "defining the ends of human life and action as well as the virtues required for becoming a fulfilled, perfect person." And the natural law is the moral underpinning in reaching that end. It establishes the norms of morality without which we would be unable to distinguish right from wrong.

For others (mostly liberals), ethics is devoid of moral absolutes. They adopt a utilitarian, amoral system based on the so-called "pleasure principle" which holds that the good society is the one providing the greatest happiness to the greatest number.

With no appeal to absolute values there are no "oughts" and as a consequence the dominant group in power has no limitations. Those with power implement whatever has political, social, or economic utility. This leads to a situation ethics – the ends justifying the means. The common good is "whatever works," as President Obama has frequently said.

This ethical approach permits a philosophy of expediency. Self-proclaimed "enlightened" Democrats who enter public life are exempt from some rules of conduct because they are the chosen ones – the elite who are called to transform America into a Utopian paradise. Because they are noble, they do not break laws or commit offenses – they only make occasional mistakes.

Republicans, on the other hand, are condemned for their transgressions – whether genuine or perceived – because they are ignoble. They enter public life for self-serving reasons and are driven by avarice and greed.

Like it or not, that's the prevailing wisdom in Washington. And we are going to have to live with it for at least four long years.

Chapter 3

Narcissist Political Religions
and Its Idols

August 12, 2009

Political Religions

In two remarkable books, *Earthly Powers* and *Sacred Causes*, British historian Michael Burleigh has traced the clash of religion and politics from the French Revolution to our own times. Burleigh shows that modern materialist creeds – Jacobinism, Fascism, Communism, and Nazism – had these common traits: They viewed man not as a person created *Imago Dei*, but as a speck within mass society devoid of freedom, self-responsibility, and conscience; and to supplant organized religions, these secularists portrayed themselves as pseudo-divine and elevated their revolutions to religious status.

The French Jacobins suppressed the Church (by 1794 only 150 of 40,000 churches were offering Mass) and replaced it with a civic religion. The Declaration of the Rights of Man was a political gospel. Baptism was redefined "as the regeneration of the French revolution begun on July 14, 1789." Communion: an association of French people "to form on earth only one family of brothers who no longer recognize or worship any idol or tyrant." Penitence: "the banishment of all those monsters . . . unworthy to inhabit the land of liberty."

To eliminate the Lord's Day, a calendar was created with ten-day weeks. Holy days were replaced with secular feast days called Virtue, Genus, Labor, Recompenses, and Opinion. Notre Dame Cathedral was converted into a "Temple of Reason." An opera singer was worshipped as the "Goddess of Liberty."

Mussolini described Fascism as "a religious conception in which man in his imminent relationship with a superior law and with an objective Will that transcends the particular individual and raises him to conscious membership of spiritual society."

Determined to destroy Italy's Catholic culture, Mussolini promoted a politics laced with religious symbols. There were mandatory oaths that affirmed the sacrificial community, consecrated political symbols, veneration of war dead and party martyrs.

Ballia, the Fascist youth movement, issued a catechism whose creed included these words: "I believe in Rome the eternal, in the mother of my country and in Italy her eldest daughter who was born in her virginal bosom. . . . I believe in the genius of Mussolini, in our holy father Fascism, in the communion of its martyrs, in the conversion of Italians and in the resurrection of the empire."

In Russia the Bolsheviks, who closed 31,000 Orthodox and Catholic churches and persecuted 10 million in the gulags for their religious beliefs, modeled themselves on the Society of Jesus and issued infallible doctrines of salvation. The Soviet nation was designed as a theocracy: the state was the administrative bureaucracy and the Party was the designer and guardian of socialist ideological orthodoxy.

Lenin's mummified body was worshipped. He was proclaimed "the apostle of world communism . . . a leader of cosmic stature, a mover of worlds . . . the chosen one."

The Nazi creed was soteriological, "a redemptive story of suffering and deliverance, a sentimental journey from misery to glory, from division to mystic unity based on the blood that linked souls." The holy of holies was the Swastika blood-stained in the failed November 1923 Munich putsch. Hitler consecrated new flags at rituals by touching them with the blood-stained one.

To overshadow the established religions, the Nazis instituted holy days honoring Hitler's birthday and the Munich putsch martyrs. Every November 18, Hitler would attend a "Last Supper" dinner in Munich, with surviving "Apostles" of the putsch. Annual rallies were held in the new Mecca, Nuremberg, the "capital city of the movement."

Reviewing the German revolution's economic materialism, racist biology, corrupt psychology and scientism, political philosopher Eric Voegelin's assessment applied to all these state religions: "Modernity without restraint."

In the aftermath of this age of guillotines, gallows, gas chambers and gulags, the secularists have continued to pursue their agenda but under the guise of good government causes. In the United States, for instance, do-gooding social theorists have elevated to religious status drives to stop over-population and pollution.

The group EarthFirst! displays an extreme form of a broad ecological current, but openly expresses some of the common elements concealed by others. For example, it insists that Western culture must be eliminated because it is responsible for "ecocide." These Eco-Warriors call for "the holiest fight of all . . . an eco-jihad."

By appealing to man's religious instincts to promote atheist ideologies, do these secularists implicitly affirm what they explicitly deny? Catholic historian Christopher Dawson, whose work influenced Burleigh, would say yes.

For Dawson, man knows by nature that there is something greater than himself and is driven to the transcendent. Religion serves man "as a bridge between the spiritual and the physical." "A culture that has by and large rejected its religion or secularized itself," Dawson argued, "has merely substituted some false religion – most likely an ideology of some kind – for its lost faith." Ideologies are merely "religious emotions divorced from religious belief."

The recently deceased philosopher Leszek Kolakowski agreed: "Mankind can never get rid of the need for religious self-identification. . . . Religion is a paramount aspect of human culture. Religious need cannot be ex-communicated from culture by rationalist incantation. Man does not live by reason alone."

Michael Burleigh has performed a great service. His books further bolster Dawson's belief that a "completely secularized civilization is inhuman in the absolute sense – hostile to human life and irreconcilable with human nature itself."

We see what secularized civilizations did in the past. Are we alert to what they are producing in the present and will in the future?

May 22, 2009

Semper Fidel

In April, seven members of the Congressional Black Caucus returned from a Cuban junket giddy over the private audience they had with ailing Communist dictator, Fidel Castro. A mesmerized Congressman Bobby Rush (D-Ill.) said "I think what really surprised me, but also endeared me to [Castro] was his keen sense of humor, his sense of history, his basic human qualities." Picture it – Castro cracking humane jokes and charming the visitors – the same Castro who over fifty years sent many Catholics, Protestants, and non-believers who did not agree with him to political prisons, quite a few of whom never returned, something almost everyone has now forgotten.

No one should be surprised by Congressman Rush's comment. He's a member of the latest generation of "useful idiots" who embrace charismatic tyrants. When Castro descended from the Cuban mountains in January 1959 and overthrew the Batista regime, he was portrayed by U.S. sympathizers as a revolutionary freedom fighter who extolled democratic virtues. Even after he abolished human rights, civil liberties, free elections, political parties, independent unions, religious and cultural organizations, and instituted political prisons and forced labor – intellectuals and progressives continued to gush over him.

During Castro's 1959 visit to the United States, 10,000 (!) members of the Harvard community greeted him on campus with a standing ovation. Novelist Norman Mailer, founder of the Fair Play for Cuba Committee, issued this proclamation: "I announce to the City of New York that you [Castro] gave all of us who are alone in this country . . . some sense there were heroes in the world. . . . It was as if the ghost of Cortez had appeared in our century riding Zapata's white horse. . . . You are the answer to the argument of commissars and statesmen that revolutions cannot last, that they turn corrupt or total or eat their own."

Mailer wasn't the only prominent cheerleader: Senator George McGovern found Castro "in private conversation at least, soft spoken, shy, sensitive." Julian Bond said that Castro's explanation of his ideological positions made him think of the "connection between socialism and Christianity." Dan Rather called him "Cuba's own Elvis"; filmmaker Oliver Stone, "very selfless and moral." Then there was singer Harry Belafonte who said: "If you believe in freedom, if you believe in justice, if you believe in democracy, you have no choice but to support Fidel Castro." It's always worth remembering these sorts of romantic delusions, because they have a way of happening over and over, with disastrous effect.

Here's the real story of the Castro era: Shortly after seizing power, Castro ordered his henchmen to infiltrate and destroy Catholic parishes. He closed Catholic universities – including his alma mater Bethlehem Jesuit College – and confiscated the property. Hundreds of priests were expelled; Catholic institutions were abolished or marginalized. Those who openly professed their faith were denied higher education and jobs and many were tossed into prison.

In his harrowing memoir of twenty-two years in a Castro prison (1960–1982), *Against All Hope*, Armando Valladares, a staunch Catholic, vividly describes how he and others endured the terror, brutality, and violence of Castro's political police as well as decades of solitary confinement, squalid living conditions, and putrid food.

Every time he wavered, Valladares thought "about the integrity of those [prison] martyrs who had died shouting '*Viva Cuba Libre!* Viva Christ the King! Down with Communism!'" "I was," he wrote, "ashamed to feel so frightened. I realized that the only way to honor the memory of those heroes was to behave with their firmness and integrity. My heart rose up to God, and I fervently prayed for Him to help me stand up to his brutality, and do what I had to do. I felt that God heard my prayer." That's the audacity of hope!

Since 1959 over 500,000 people have spent time in a Cuban

gulag. The authoritative *Black Book of Communism: Crimes, Terror, Repression* – written by a team of French intellectuals – reports that there have been 15,000–20,000 prisoners of conscience; 12,000–15,000 political prisoners; and 15,000–17,000 prisoners shot. Over 2 million Cubans, out of a population of 11 million, "voted with oars" and settled in other countries. In 1994 alone, over 7,000 attempting to escape died at sea. When confronted with these facts, Castro replied: "From our point of view, we have no human-rights problem – there have been no 'disappeareds' here, there have been no tortures here, there have been no murderers here . . . torture has never been committed, a crime has never been committed."

As is happening with much else of vital historical value, the real story seems to be disappearing down the memory hole. The Organization of American States is dedicated to promoting democratic principles in Latin America and holds "that adherence by any members . . . to Marxism-Leninism is incompatible with the inter-American systems . . . and breaks the unity and solidarity of the hemisphere." Yet it is ready to accept Cuba as a member.

Rejecting what he calls "stale Cold War arguments," President Obama has called for a new friendly relationship with Cuba that will include the lifting of the embargo if some political prisoners are released and Cuban taxes on remittances from the United States are reduced.

The reaction to this kinder, gentler approach towards Cuba? Fidel Castro, the last Cold War thug, poked Obama in the eye. In a recent article, Castro accused the president of showing signs of "superficiality" and made it clear that Obama had "no right to suggest that Cuba make even small concessions."

Plus ça change, plus c'est la même chose.

October 28, 2009

Sixty Years of Maoism

Throughout October there's been plenty of fussing over the six-tieth anniversary of the founding of the People's Republic of China. Editorials world-wide have saluted China's growing economic and political influence. The Empire State Building was lit up in red and yellow to commemorate the occasion. *New York Times* columnist Thomas L. Friedman described the totalitarian regime as *enlightened*: "One-party autocracy cer-tainly has its drawbacks. But when it is led by a reasonably en-lightened group of people, as China is today, it can also have great advantages. That one party can just impose the politically difficult but critically important policies needed to move a so-ciety forward in the twenty-first century."

In Washington, White House Director of Communications Anita Dunn praised Mao Tse-tung's political philosophy and called him a great defender of individualism. And Barack Obama, fearing to offend China, committed the most cowardly presidential act since President Ford declined to meet Nobel laureate Solzhenitsyn in 1975, by refusing to see the 1989 Nobel Peace Prize winner who has been fighting Chinese oppression on his Tibetan people for half a century – the Dalai Lama.

Meanwhile, the Chinese celebrated by marching tens of thousands of troops through Tiananmen Square, flaunting their latest military hardware, recruiting 800,000 spies to root out po-tential troublemakers and "inviting" would-be Chinese spec-tators to stay away from the festivities. People who lived on the streets that crossed the square were ordered not to open the windows or to stand on balconies to watch the ceremonies.

Sixty years of Chinese communist rule should be mourned, not celebrated. Contrary to the media-fueled image of Mao as a gentle philosopher and great freedom fighter, he was actually a degenerate mass murderer who ruthlessly suppressed all human rights. In their remarkable biography, *Mao: The Un-known Story*, Jung Chang and Jon Halliday revealed that Mao grew up not as an oppressed hard working peasant dedicated to fighting injustice, but as a loafer who took a job as a Communist International Soviet agent to receive "a comfortable berth as a subsidized professional revolutionary."

Mao enthusiastically adopted Lenin's most violent terrorist techniques because he was a vile bloodthirsty thug. From 1920 to 1976 Mao murdered more people than Hitler and Stalin combined – 70 million Chinese. The "Great Famine" (1958–1961) in which 40 million perished was a direct result of Mao's farm collectivization policies. To eliminate tens of millions of imagined enemies he ordered the "Great Leap Forward" (1958) and the "Cultural Revolution" (1966–1968) which he privately referred to as the "Great Purge."

Mao attempted to control every form of social intercourse. Merely having a dinner party or the use of humor or sarcasm could be – and were – deemed criminal activities that warranted the death penalty. And he was proud of these policies: Mao told his fellow gangsters at the 1958 party conference that they should welcome, not fear, party policies that cause people to die.

Mao ruthlessly suppressed centuries-old Catholic missions. His persecution of Catholics began long before he took over the government in 1949. In the 1920s, 30s, and 40s, Mao's Red armies roamed through Chinese provinces torturing and murdering scores of priests and nuns. In 1947, for instance, eighteen Cistercian monks at Yang Kia Ping were jailed and their monastery was looted. All died from endless interrogations, beatings, and brainwashing.

The Red Chinese were not content with suppressing the Church. They dumped Catholics into re-education camps and used harsh psychological measures that included physical and mental torture to convert them to Marxism. If the education treatments failed, it was hoped that recalcitrant pupils would go mad or commit suicide.

In recent decades, the Communists continued to persecute China's 5 million Catholics. After the 1989 anti-government demonstrations in Tiananmen Square, there were crackdowns on the underground Church. "House Churches" were destroyed and priests were arrested. Also, Catholic women were forced to have abortions or were sterilized to comply with China's "one-child policy."

In May 2007, Pope Benedict XVI released a letter to the Catholics of China which dealt with the relationship between Church and State. The pontiff reaffirmed there was only one Church which included both the unofficial underground one and the government-recognized Patriotic Catholic Church. He respectfully called for religious freedom and constructive dialogue to overcome disagreements.

The pope's pleas appear to have fallen on deaf ears. Priests and bishops are still imprisoned and the faithful continue to be physically abused by government officials.

In May 2008, on the feast of Our Lady, Help of Christians, Pope Benedict held a worldwide day of prayer for the Church in China. However, Chinese Catholic pilgrims who travelled to Mary Helper of Christians Shrine near Shanghai to participate in the day of prayer were denied access to the consecrated grounds by the police.

America's elitist intellectual and political classes have a distorted view of today's China. Contrary to their revisionist claims, China's people still lack basic freedoms and their state-run economic system is built on the graves of millions of victims of Mao's depravity.

November 17, 2010

Hugo Chavez: Anti-Catholic, Narcissist, Leninist

When Hugo Chavez was sworn in as president of Venezuela in February 1997, he was hailed as the true successor to Latin American freedom fighter, Simon Bolivar. Notables including Sean Penn, Harry Belafonte, Oliver Stone, and Noam Chomsky shouted from rooftops that Chavez was a visionary who would restore prosperity and return power to the people. And they applauded his claim that the United States is "the most evil regime that has ever existed."

These useful idiots have turned a blind eye to the fact that Chavez is a depraved Marxist totalitarian whose heroes are Fidel Castro, Che Guevara, Mahmoud Ahmadinejad of Iran, Robert Mugabe of Zimbabwe, and Hezbollah leader Hassan Nasrallah. They have also ignored that he supports global terrorism, has provided sanctuary to the Colombian terrorist group FARC, and has pledged "that nothing will stop us" from acquiring nuclear power.

A misogynist who claimed former U.S. Secretary of State Condoleezza Rice found him irresistible, Chavez has been described by his long-term mistress and mother of his child as a "typical narcissist dictator." "Ego" Chavez, as dissenters refer to him, has been called "Der Narziss von Caracas" by *Die Zeit* foreign correspondent Reiner Luyken and a "Narcissist-Leninist" by *The Miami Herald* columnist Andres Oppenheimer.

Since taking office Chavez has destroyed what was considered the most stable Latin American democratic country. A 300-page 2010 report issued by the Inter-American Human Rights Commission accused Chavez of massive violations of human rights, the destruction of democratic principles such as the separation of powers, judicial review of acts of state, and the rule of law over the will of the president. The report concluded that there are "persistent threats and violations of human rights involving political participation, freedom of thought and expression, right to life, personal security and personal integrity and liberty."

During his tenure, national literacy has gone up only 1 percent and crime is rampant. Homicide rates have increased 90 percent between 1998 and 2005 and 91 percent of murders are never solved. At 57 murders per 100,000 people, Venezuela's homicide rate is the world's highest. Not included in these statistics are the thousands who are killed annually "resisting authority."

The Index of Economic Freedom study of 157 countries places Venezuela in 148th place. Transparency International rates Venezuela as one of the world's most corrupt nations.

Throughout his reign of terror, the major thorn in Chavez's side has been the hierarchy of Venezuela's Roman Catholic Church. Venezuela, a nation of 25 million, is 90 percent Catholic and recent polling indicates that 80 percent of the population is supportive of the Church and regards it as trustworthy.

The bishops have instructed their flocks that Chavez's brand of socialism is not compatible with the social teachings of the Church. In October 2006, Archbishop Diego Rafael Padrón Sanchez of Cumana declared: "Chavez's so-called twenty-first century socialism has already been polarizing the country for seven years. People are for him or against him, but nevertheless, they have remained poor."

In 2007, the bishops opposed Chavez's constitutional reform referendum that would have given him dictatorial powers. The proposals, they said, were undemocratic and a massive attack on civil rights, particularly freedom of expression.

Venezuela's seminarians also refused to stand on the sidelines. In an open letter to the bishop's conference, they stated that the "reforms" were "morally unacceptable" and "irreconcilable with the Christian faith and its view of man and society." As for Chavez's plan to stifle dissent, the seminarians expressed support for those who act and speak "in accordance with their conscience" and condemned "as a threat to democracy when violent physical or verbal means are used against those who express their views openly."

After the constitutional referendum was defeated, 51 percent to 49 percent, Chavez went ballistic and condemned the bishops, priests, and seminarians as fomenting rebellion and "talking nonsense." He ordered them to read "Marx, Lenin, and the Sermon on the Mount to discover the true inspiration of socialism."

To break the influence of the Church, Chavez designed a law that ended traditional government subsidies to Catholic schools and ended the right of children to receive religious education in government-run schools. Cardinal Jorge Urosa condemned the measures and warned that he would continue to vigorously oppose Chavez's "socialism of the twenty-first century that was proving to be similar to old style communist regimes."

The bishops have also opposed Chavez's fifteen-year plan to integrate Cuba, Venezuela, Honduras, Nicaragua, Bolivia, and Ecuador under one socialist-government umbrella.

In July of this year, Chavez, in an address to the National Assembly, denounced Cardinal Urosa as a "troglodyte" who is "unworthy of calling himself Cardinal." Looking directly at the papal nuncio, a guest in the audience, Chavez said: "Nuncio, please tell [His] Holiness that as long as we have these bishops we feel that we will be far away from the hierarchy of the church. . . . This battle is not over. . . . I feel sorrow when the Cardinal talks like a troglodyte and he tries to scare people about communism. We do not deserve such a Cardinal."

Cardinal Urosa reacted immediately stating that Chavez's ultimate goal is "to impose a socialist-Marxist system in the country to control all sectors. . . . A dictatorship led by the [ruling] elite."

Despite threats and violence against the Church, the bishops and priests have refused to back off. Cardinal Urosa continues to battle the regime even after a government gang, La

Esquina Caliente, physically assaulted him. The people of Venezuela are fortunate that their fearless Church leaders have prevented Chavez's bully-state from totally enslaving them. American Catholics – and everyone of goodwill – should support them in this all-too-familiar struggle.

January 13, 2010

Modern Scoundrels

In 1907, St. Pius X asserted in the encyclical *Pascendi*: "It is pride which fills Modernists with that self-assurance by which they consider themselves and pose as the rule for all. It is pride which puffs them up with that vainglory which allows them to regard themselves as the sole possessors of knowledge, and makes them say, elated and inflated with presumption, *We are not as the rest of men*, and which, lest they should seem as other men, leads them to embrace and to devise novelties even of the most absurd kind. . . . It is owing to their pride that they seek to be the reformers of others while they forget to reform themselves."

This is the kind of remark that, of course, embarrasses a certain kind of Catholic, especially since Vatican II. In 2007, on the centenary of *Pascendi*, many of them not only deplored such sentiments, they labored to make it appear that the encyclical's very premises were absurd. But are they?

Modernists come in a variety of kinds, to be sure, and Catholics know that we are all sinners. Still, the evidence is in that departing from ancient philosophical and theological wisdom has, as Pius X knew, serious consequences.

A case in point: the Hungarian leftist and intellectual Arthur Koestler (1905–1983) has been much in the news lately thanks to the publication of Michael Scammell's monumental 700-page biography, *Koestler: The Literary and Political Odyssey of a Twentieth Century Skeptic.*

Koestler, who wrote thirty books in his lifetime, is best remembered for repudiating his Communist Party membership in *The God That Failed*, a collection of essays that he helped edit, and for describing the horrors of Stalin's purges in his 1940 novel *Darkness at Noon*. So far so good. But he shed his Communist faith, and adopted a different modernist one. Later in life, in such works as *Beyond Reductionism* and *The Ghost in the Machine*, he disputed the claims of scientific materialists that man was nothing more than a bundle of atoms – by appealing to parapsychology.

This shift was not wholly for the better. Koestler also had a dark side that dabbling in the paranormal did not restrain. He was a nasty, miserable, cruel man who mistreated his mother, refused even to meet his illegitimate daughter, and was accused of rape by a friend's wife. Koestler admitted that growing up he was "admired for my brains and detested for my character," and wrote to the woman who was to be his second wife, "without an element of initial rape there is no delight." A narcissist to the end, he did not object to his young and healthy third wife's committing suicide together with him.

No one should be surprised by these revelations. Many high-minded modernists, who publicly lectured the human race on how to manage its affairs, have privately been lowlifes who believed they were exempt from the usual rules of civility. Here are a few more examples of secular titans whose personal lives consisted of lies, hatred, selfishness, and sexual perversion:

Jean-Jacques Rousseau (1712–1778) virtually invented the radical modern critique of existing societies, blaming everything on social influences and exonerating individuals, especially himself. He therefore sought to alter human behavior by creating a social contract giving the state a claim to represent the General Will. Rousseau's totalitarian state would, in the name of humanitarianism, coerce citizens to submit to a new order that promised to regenerate mankind and eliminate perceived injustices, miseries, and disorders.

Rousseau believed he was a compassionate servant of the people directing mankind toward a higher state of being. "I feel too superior to hate," he declared. "I love myself too much to hate anybody." But in fact, he was a self-centered scoundrel who treated people like dirt. He condemned his five illegitimate children at birth to the dreaded Paris orphanage system in which the life expectancy for two-thirds of the inmates was less than a year. I.W. Allen has described Rousseau as a "masochist, exhibitionist, neurasthenic, hypochondriac, onanist . . . incipient paranoiac, narcissistic introvert . . . a kleptomaniac, infantilist, irritable, and miserly."

Karl Marx (1818–1883), was a heavy drinking, bad tempered, disorderly slob who browbeat family, colleagues, and followers (he also had an affair with the housemaid). A rabid anti-Semite, he declared that if the world was to be saved, it must emancipate "itself from hucksterism and money, and thus from the real and practical Judaism." "Marx," Mikhail Bakunin observed, "does not believe in God, but he believes much in himself and makes everyone serve himself. His heart is not full of love, but of bitterness, and he has very little sympathy for the human race." To judge by results, leaders of Marxist regimes seem to have followed the master's life as much as his ideology.

Bertrand Russell (1872–1970), a philosopher and intellectual aristocrat, who made himself publicly notorious as an anti-nuclear crusader, was in private a dedicated lecher who despised and pitied average people and felt above the rules of society, except when he found them useful.

Jean-Paul Sartre (1905–1980), the super egoist who, when not overindulging in alcohol and barbiturates, had long-term companion Simone de Beauvoir serve as his sexual procuress. Sartre and Beauvoir loudly pursued Nazi collaborators after World War II, but during the Nazi occupation they themselves got along fine with the authorities and lived very well indeed. Their books continued to be published and their plays produced.

These modernists may have loved mankind in the abstract, but in reality despised actual persons. Was Pius X wrong in observing that "they seek to be the reformers of others while they forget to reform themselves"? Koestler and his heartless confreres were guilty of the same sin that brought down Satan, and Adam and Eve – pride.

January 27, 2010

The Big Lie Continues

We hear a little about Muslim persecution of Christians these days, though not much. But is anyone aware of the much larger and continuing evil presence that violates the rights and very lives of Catholics and other believers in our world? It's called Communism, and in China, Vietnam, Cuba, and a gaggle of wannabe Marxist dictatorships, this murderous ideology continues to generate high body counts and gulags for the Christians of the world while the mainstream media and prominent intellectuals hardly seem to notice.

There is ample precedent for this lack of interest going back even before the fall of the Berlin Wall and the dissolution of Communism in Eastern Europe. Throughout the twentieth century, the progressive intelligentsia was sympathetic to the idea that Marxist-controlled states would eventually give birth to an international utopian community. To maintain this view, they defended, denied, or overlooked the crimes against humanity committed by Lenin, Stalin, Mao, Castro, Pol Pot, and their henchmen.

Even as the very foundations of the Iron Curtain were crumbling in the late 1980s, many leftist thinkers continued to promote Communist "truth." For instance, one year before the fall of the Berlin Wall, America's oldest left-wing journal, *The Nation*, refusing to face the harsh facts about the Soviet totalitarian menace, toed the party line by condemning the Center for Democracy, created by U.S. citizens to aid the only independent publication in the U.S.S.R., *Glasnost*.

One European who had the courage to expose the lies was the late French philosopher-journalist Jean-Francois Revel (1924–2006). This World War II resistance fighter and Social Democrat fearlessly fought the ideological bullies of his time. For him, they functioned "as a machine to destroy information even at the price of making assertions in clear contradiction of the evidence." And they still do. As Paul Valery, a

French poet, once observed, "everything changes but the avant-garde."

Revel swam against the French intellectual tide by arguing that evil is inherent in Communism's DNA. History, he believed, proved that as a governing system, it was never economically viable and retarded social justice: "Incarceration camps and prisons, show trials, murderous purges and deliberately induced famines have accompanied each and every Communist regime from beginning to end, without exception."

The global left, of course, despised Revel. In a series of trenchant works, *The Totalitarian Temptation* (1976), *How Democracies Perish* (1983), *The Flight From Truth* (1991), and *Anti-Americanism* (2003), Revel assaulted those "who openly and on principle allow the annihilation of whole masses of humanity . . . to secure the realization of the Communist ideal." He denounced leftists who, in the name of progress, yielded to the *totalitarian temptation* and became accomplices to political crimes.

In *Last Exit to Utopia*, a book of his just translated and published posthumously, Revel gives socialist apologists his last dig. Revel makes the case that many leftist intellectuals have been in a state of denial since the death of the Soviet leviathan. They cannot admit they were intellectually wrong or morally compromised. Communism, they still insist, was an engine of social justice that had good intentions. Genuine Communists tried to create a good society that would save the masses from "enslavement to consumerism." Revel calls this behavior "voluntary blindness;" ideologues ignoring or deforming truth to rationalize their apriori schemes.

To maintain the fiction and to take the spotlight off their shortcomings, these leftists have aggressively pursued a "take no prisoners" offensive strategy. The root of all evil they insist is "savage capitalism" and the devils who promote this depraved system are Americans. Critics of Communist regimes are "simplistic" and "obsessive" mean-spirited right-wing reactionaries or just plain old fascists.

Scholarly works that document Communist oppression are dismissed as "nostalgia for the Cold War." "Why drag out that old stuff?" is the typical reaction from the leftist chorus. "Haven't we heard it all before? Let's move on." American leftist elites employed this approach in their failed attempt to stop the acclaimed Yale University Press *Annals of Communism* series which publishes previously inaccessible documents from Soviet state and party archives.

The most vicious outcry was against the 800-page compendium detailing the crimes of Communist regimes worldwide, *The Black Book of Communism: Crimes, Terror, Repression.* Furious leftists used every vicious tactic to discredit the findings of the five French authors that over 100 million people were murdered for belonging to political parties, churches, or some hated social class. Critics pressured and intimidated the contributors – even threatening to get them fired from their academic posts – if they did not recant.

One delusional protester, the Marxist Jacques Rossi, who actually served time in the Gulag, defended the prison system claiming these Soviet camps were fine institutions that "served as a laboratory for the Soviet regime in order to create an ideal society: to compel obedience and indoctrinate."

Revel boldly rejected these cover-ups. Western ideologues, he declared, "may have no blood on their hands; but their pens are dripping with it." Contrary to their claims, totalitarian states, unlike capitalist democracies, *must* commit crimes to survive. Recent actions by remaining Marxist regimes confirm his thesis: North Korea's Communist masters have systematically starved over 3 million of their people. In Tibet 1.2 million people – 20 percent of the total population – have been eliminated under China's occupation of that nation. And in China itself, the regime has set up a subservient Patriotic Catholic Church to keep Catholics from following the real Church with its head in the Vatican.

Communism, writes Revel, "promises abundance and engenders misery; promises liberty and imposes servitude. . .

promises respect for human life and then perpetuates mass executions; promises the creation of a 'new man,' but instead fossilizes him." Yet by using "evil in the name of good," Revel observes, this failed experiment tragically continues to attract "angelic accomplices, in the name of ideals they have shamelessly trampled underfoot."

February 24, 2010

Pluralism – or Relativism

This past year, secularists have been celebrating the centennial of the birth of one of their ideological heroes, Oxford don Sir Isaiah Berlin (1909–1997).

Born in Riga, Professor Berlin and his family escaped Bolshevik persecution and settled in Britain in 1921. He was educated at Oxford and spent his career teaching there, was knighted in 1957, and wrote over twenty books on philosophical, political, and cultural subjects.

Although Berlin is more talked about than read, he is still viewed by the secularists as one of the leading liberal intellectuals of the twentieth century. He is remembered, foremost, as an erudite wit, one of the illuminati who turn clever phrases at exclusive soirees. Berlin is also honored as a practical philosopher because he embraced what he called a "pluralism of values" and frowned upon those who subscribed to absolute and transcendent standards.

In his famous 1958 essay, "Two Concepts of Liberty," Berlin dismissed truth and certainty in these words: "Indeed, the very desire for guarantees that our values are eternal and secure in some objective heaven is perhaps only a craving for the certainties of childhood or the absolute values of our primitive past." In other words, anyone who argues for universal truths is a childish Neanderthal.

Despite this position, Berlin still insisted he was not a relativist. "I do not say 'I like my coffee with milk and you like it without; I am in favor of kindness and you prefer concentration camps.'" But he never made clear the basis of this claim. For all his sophistication, like we lesser lights, Berlin can't have his cake and also eat it. To deny there is an absolute (i.e., a natural law) that supersedes all statutes, that abrogates perverted legal orders, is to make death camps legally permissible, and historically led to them.

A leading intellectual proponent of legal positivism, Hans

Kelsen, put it this way: "The legal order of totalitarian states authorizes their Governments to confine in concentration camps persons whose opinions, religion, or race they do not like; to force them to perform any kind of labor, even to kill them. Such measures may be morally or violently condemned; but they cannot be considered as taking place outside the legal order of those states. . . . We may regret it but we cannot deny that it was law."

In Nazi Germany, for instance, Hitler was legally able to obtain the power to fashion the Final Solution because the regime rejected eternal, immutable values. Hitler legally became a law unto himself – with quite predictable results. His authority was confirmed equally by appointed judges and elected legislators, and he was able to boast, "We stand absolutely as hard as granite on the ground of legality."

Pope Benedict, who lived under the Nazi regime, has said that, at least in this, Hitler was quite right. Law in Nazi Germany, Benedict has written, "was constantly castigated and placed in opposition to so-called popular feeling. The Führer was successively declared the only source of law and, as a result, absolute power replaced law. The denigration of law never serves the causes of liberty, but is always an instrument of dictatorship."

To convict the Nazis at the Nuremberg trial of crimes against humanity, the prosecution had to reject the moral and legal relativism promoted by Isaiah Berlin and to invoke the natural law. Peter Kreeft has written that the Nuremberg trial "assumed that such universal moral law really existed."

Robert H. Jackson, an associate justice of the Supreme Court who served as America's chief counsel at Nuremberg, flatly stated: "We do not accept the paradox that legal responsibility should be least where the power is the greatest." Justice Jackson liked to recall English jurist Edward Coke's rebuke of James I's assertion of royal authority: "A King," Coke reminded the monarch, "is still under God and law."

In his closing argument, Jackson made this plea, "I cannot

subscribe to the perverted reasoning that society may advance and strengthen the rule of law by the expenditure of morally innocent lives but that progress in law may never be made at the price of morally guilty lives."

It is interesting that the standard used by the world to condemn the Nazis at Nuremberg was the same one Jefferson asked the "candid world" to use in vindicating America's Revolution. Had these judgments been based solely upon legal positivism or relativism, such vicious men as Hitler, Eichmann, and Himmler might have been considered law-abiding, and such virtuous men as Washington, Adams, and Jefferson might have been labeled outlaws.

By rejecting the natural law and subscribing to a "pluralism of values," Isaiah Berlin and his secularist admirers are intellectual prisoners of what Pope Benedict has called the "dictatorship of relativism that does not recognize anything as definitive and whose ultimate goal consists solely of one's ego and desires."

As history has shown, this is not only a private question – as we are often told – but leads, often quite quickly, to the most serious public consequences.

August 11, 2010

On Hobbes' *Leviathan*

In the July 14 edition of *The Wall Street Journal*, Professor Jeffrey
Collins of Queen's University, Ontario, claimed that Thomas
Hobbes' seventeenth-century political treatise *Leviathan*, which
laid the ideological foundation for the omnipotent state, is popular reading these days.

"Today," the professor wrote, "*Leviathan* is considered one
of the greatest works of political theory ever written. . . . The
very title of Hobbes' masterpiece [which is standard reading
in most colleges] has become a byword for the modern
state." And he agreed with introductory comments in the new
Yale edition of *Leviathan* that Hobbes comes across as "our
philosophical contemporary" and has made "very deep in-
roads" into our thinking.

If Collins is right, America is in deep trouble. That's because Hobbes, the father of modern statism and the first advocate of totalitarianism, rejected the insights of Aristotle and St.
Thomas Aquinas that man by his nature is a social animal who
forms society by the demands and impulses of his rational nature working through free will. Hobbes also dismissed the notion that human reason possesses the power to discover the
natural law.

Instead, Hobbes postulated that the state is founded on
man's right of self-preservation. He assumed that man is naturally in a state of complete liberty and is driven only by his
passions and desires. "Every man for his part, calleth that
which pleaseth and is delightful to himself, good; and that evil
which displeaseth him. . . . And as we call good and evil the
things that please and displease; so we call goodness and bad-
ness the qualities or powers whereby they do it." Since each
person is completely free to do as he wishes, each person is free
to violate the freedom of other people. Hobbesian man is vain,
contentious, revengeful, and self-seeking; his primitive anti-so-
cial "state of nature" leads to a condition of constant warfare

and hostility. Man becomes "a wolf to man." There is a "war of all against all" with "no justice because there is no law." The natural origin of the state discovered by the great ancients and medievals is replaced with the contractual theory of the state invented by Hobbes.

Due to their impulse for self-preservation and the realization of the incompatibility of competing interests, Hobbes holds that men come together by compact (the general will) and cede their natural freedom to a sovereign who makes and enforces law. According to Hobbes:

> The only way to erect such a common power . . . is to confer all their power and strength on one man, or upon one assembly of men, that may reduce all their wills by plurality of voices, unto one will. . . . This is more than consent, or concord: it is a real unity of them all, in one and the same person, made by covenant of every man with every man. *I authorize and give up my right of governing myself, to this man or to this assembly of men, on this condition, that thou give up the right to him, and authorize all his actions in like manner.* This done, the multitude so united in one person, is called a commonwealth. . . . For by this authority, given him by every particular man in the commonwealth, he hath the use of so much power and strength conferred on him, *that by terror thereof,* he is enabled to perform the wills of them all, to peace at home, and mutual aid against their enemies abroad. [Italics added.]

The populace irrevocably conveys its liberties to the state, its private judgments to an absolute sovereign. To control the passions and judgments of the populace the sovereign has terrifying power, since, in Hobbes' words, "covenants without the sword are but words and of no strength to secure a man." The head of state is absolutely indivisible and inalienable, and he defines the "natural law" as he sees fit, which means natural law is ignored.

In Hobbes' doctrines there is no room for the concept of

subsidiarity or the family as a necessary institution in society. In effect, Hobbes knew only the harsh antagonism of individual against the state, a conflict he believed the state must win. The noted Catholic philosopher Heinrich Rommen argued that Hobbes also "lacked an understanding of the particular nature of the Church as a 'perfect' society: it became either a department of the state or a spiritual free fellowship, not an institution."

Hobbes' *Leviathan* may be currently popular in Barack Obama's Washington where, in broad daylight, people whom historian Richard Hofstadter called "totalitarian liberals" employ illiberal means to achieve so-called liberal reforms. These authoritarians of the left, according to Hofstadter, often embrace "hatred as a form of creed" in the pursuit of their goals.

Professor Collins hit on this in his *Journal* article: "When pundits such as Thomas Friedman decry 'broken government' and fawn over China's 'enlightened' response to global warming or are puzzled by Americans' widespread resistance to Obamacare, one wonders if the Hobbesian within the liberal breast is stirring."

Proponents of a Hobbesian state should be feared because they are determined to transform American culture according to their current view of its best interests, and the means for the changes they would effect is raw power. To them liberty means obedience to the uncertain will of the elite, even in matters of life and death. To them, the modern liberal state, not God, is absolute.

November 25, 2009

Dr. Singer's Immodest Proposal

In an October 26, 2009, op-ed in the *New York Daily News*, Princeton University professor of bioethics Peter Singer applauded New York's nanny-state measures (i.e., abolition of trans-fats in restaurants, high cigarette taxes, and similar fashionable causes) but complained that government policymakers were ignoring what he referred to as "the cow in the room."

To stop people who are meat eaters from killing fellow animals, the planet, and themselves, Singer calls on state and local governments to impose a "50 percent tax on the retail value of all meat." Such action, he believes, will not only diminish meat consumption, improve the lives of cows, pigs, and chickens, lower health insurance premiums, and bring down the price of grain and soybeans; it would be "a highly effective way of reducing our greenhouse gas emissions and avoiding catastrophic climate change."

One should not dismiss Dr. Singer's tax plan as a satirical Jonathan Swift-like *Modest Proposal* – he is quite serious. Singer, who believes in the equality of all sentient life forms, finds man to be an appalling beast because he kills and eats the flesh of his equals – cows, pigs and chickens. (About non-human animals who eat other animals sometimes including us, the professor seems to have far less to say.) In an 1986 essay titled "All Animals are Equal," Singer contends that the last remaining discrimination is speciesism, which holds that one species is superior to another. Singer demanded "that we extend to other species the basic principle of equality that most of us recognize should be extended to all members of our own species." In fact, Singer demotes some humans by insisting that the pig has more consciousness and therefore is entitled to more rights than fetuses or sick people.

Singer's ability to make these arguments may be traced back to seventeenth-century reductionism, which measures everything in the universe *quantitatively*. Hence, man is not a person, he is only another thing.

By strictly restricting science to mean various versions of materialism, physicists, political scientists, economists, and psychologists must treat man and beast alike as machines differing only in degree of complexity. Thanks to such "scientific" reductionism, psychology especially is no longer the study of man as a spiritual being possessing body and soul, but is merely biology, the study of cells. Biology is then reduced to the study of organic chemistry. Chemistry is reduced to the study of physics in which, finally, man is an organism in which atoms swirl and quanta pop in and out of existence aimlessly.

Since all living matter, human and not, is reduced to a cell or chemical compound, the mechanists conclude that there is no difference between man and brute; that empirical evidence alone constitutes the knowledge of the phenomenon called man; that there is no "objective" existence of mind, consciousness, and the soul; that human freedom is illusion; that there is no human nature which is not malleable to techniques of design, development, and control.

Accepting these notions, Singer concludes that because man and beast both suffer, they are therefore equal. There is no sanctity of life, only quality of life. In the journal *Pediatrics*, Singer wrote in 1983, "if we compare a severely defective human infant with a nonhuman animal, a dog or a pig for example, we often find the nonhuman to have superior capacities. . . . If we can put aside the obsolete and erroneous notion of the sanctity of all human life, we may start to look at human life as it really is: the quality of life that each human being has or can achieve." Arguing that man is substantially different than the cow because he is created in the image of God is, according to Singer, merely a fine phrase that is "the last resource of those who have run out of argument." This mentality permits Singer to conclude that there is no significant difference between human slavery and cattle ranching.

For Singer, abortion, infanticide and euthanasia should be

mandatory in order to relieve society of those beings whose quality of life are not perfect – be they pre-born, young, or old. For instance, when the U.S. Supreme Court ruled in *Cruzan v. Director, Missouri Department of Health* (1990) that artificially supplied foods and liquids could be terminated because they are nothing more than "life-support systems," the jubilant Singer wrote, "The lives of such patients are of no benefit to them, and so doctors may lawfully stop feeding them to end their lives. With this decision the law has ended its unthinking commitment to the preservation of human life that is a mere biological existence. . . . In doing so they have shifted the boundary between what is and what is not murder. . . . Now, conduct intended to end life is lawful."

Today, to impose his *Weltanschauung*, Singer calls for taxing meat eaters; tomorrow he'll call for oppressive taxes on the incomes of people who are under the illusion that it is only humane to care for the sick and the elderly.

Chapter 4

New York Political Narcissists

November 5, 2010

Albany's Behavior Reaches New Lows

Twelve days before the election, New York Inspector General Joseph Fisch shocked the political establishment by releasing a no-holds-barred report on the corrupt bidding process that awarded the Aqueduct video slot contract to a blatantly unqualified consortium, Aqueduct Entertainment Group.

Fisch, a former judge and prosecutor, found that the selection of AEG by Gov. David Paterson, Assembly Speaker Sheldon Silver and Senate President Malcolm Smith "created a politically dominated process antithetical to the public interest and contrary to acceptable procurement practices."

The 308-page Fisch report stated that heavy lobbying and major contributions to the Democratic State Senate Campaign Committee and individual Democratic senators had cast "a taint on the motives behind the Senate leadership's support of AEG."

The report alleges that Senate Democratic Leader John Sampson impeded the IG's investigation, gave evasive and misleading testimony and leaked confidential information during the selection process to AEG's lobbyist. And, AEG complied with Sampson's request to hire developer Don Cogville.

The probe also revealed:

- Paterson ignored expert advice that AEG was not qualified;
- Sen. Smith pushed for AEG despite ties to its investors;
- Sen. Eric Adams advocated for AEG despite knowledge of the consortium's shortcomings;
- Senate Secretary Angelo Aponte improperly served as a "conduit of information" to AEG;
- Democratic consultant Hank Sheinkopf and Paterson's former top aide David Johnson pleaded the Fifth Amendment, stating their rights against self-incrimination;
- Former state Sen. Carl Andrews, now a lobbyist, procured inside information and memos concerning Aqueduct bids.

Reviewing the scope of the scandal which included leaks, self-dealing and favoritism to fix the outcome of the bidding process, Fisch said, "As one who has devoted an entire career spanning over half a century to public service, and as a taxpayer and resident of New York, I am outraged and profoundly saddened by the conduct throughout this process by the people who hold a responsibility to service the public, a responsibility that they betrayed."

Albany potentates have reached these corrupt lows because of a warped definition of ethics. For them ethics is devoid of moral absolutes, that is, norms of morality by which one distinguishes right from wrong. They can rationalize illicit behavior because they have adopted a utilitarian, amoral system based on the so-called "pleasure principle" which holds that achieving what is best for oneself is all that matters.

With no appeal to absolute values there are no "oughts," and as a consequence many dominant politicians believe there are no limitations on their political behavior. Such people implement whatever has political utility. This leads to situational ethics – the ends justifying the means.

This "philosophy of expediency" ethical approach permits pols to exempt themselves from some rules of conduct. Because they perceive themselves as entitled nobility, they do not break laws or commit offenses, they only make occasional mistakes.

Hence, no one should have been surprised by Sampson's remorseless reaction to Fisch's charges: "Mistakes were made at various levels of government, and we must collectively learn a lesson." This remark proves that Sampson is a narcissist incapable of grasping they were more than mistakes; there was the breach of trust his constituents bestowed on him and possibly a breach of state law he swore to uphold. IG Fisch correctly concluded that Sampson and his political cronies based their award on a "militant indifference to the public good."

The Fisch report confirms the cynical approach to governing that dominates Albany. One can only hope it serves as the catalyst that enables Governor-elect Cuomo to bring to a close the era of "anything goes."

August 7, 2007

Steamroller Spitzer

Thanks to twelve years of Republican Governor George Pataki's insouciant leadership, in November 2006 New Yorkers gave Democrat Eliot Spitzer 69% of their votes – the largest majority in the state's history.

Running as a centrist, Spitzer supported fiscal restraint, no new taxes, charter schools, and pledged that "day one everything changes."

In January, plenty changed but not for the best; Governor Spitzer discarded his cloak of moderation, relentlessly pursued a radical liberal agenda and proved to be a blustering bully.

The governor's first budget proposal called for state spending to increase 7.8%, three times the inflation rate. Spitzer, who as New York's Attorney General was known as the "scourge of Wall Street," now cowered to the state legislature's old guard and settled for a whopping 9% jump in expenditures to get a budget passed by the April 1st deadline.

Spitzer, the tough guy who promised to open the budget negotiating process, was mugged behind the capital's closed doors. His sham "reform" budget contained billions for special interests, pork for legislators, entitlements for unions and the health care cartel. The Division of Budget's analysis of the spending plan projected out-year deficits of $3.3 billion in 2008, $5.5 billion 2009 and $7.3 billion in 2010.

Reviewing this fiscal mess, Republican Assembly leader James Tedisco concluded: "The record $122 billion budget spends too much, borrows too much, taxes too much and reforms too little."

In his first months in office, Spitzer also moved to implement his leftist cultural agenda.

Shortly after the U.S. Supreme Court upheld the partial birth abortion ban, the governor announced he was introducing legislation "to enshrine the protections of *Roe v. Wade* into New York State law." "Even if the Supreme Court does not understand the law, we do," Spitzer declared. "New York will continue to be a beacon of civil rights and protector of women's rights."

On April 27, Governor Spitzer proposed legislation to legalize same-sex marriage. Referring to gay marriage as a "simple moral imperative," he described his stand as a "statement of principle that I believe in, and I want to begin that dynamic."

During his two terms as New York's Attorney General, Spitzer's self-righteous bullying and uncontrollable temper were legendary. On one occasion he told former General Electric C.E.O. Jack Welch that "he's going to put a spike through [New York Stock Exchange Director Kenneth Langone's] heart." John Whitehead, former Goldman Sachs Chairman wrote in a December 2005 *Wall Street Journal* op-ed that Spitzer threatened him after he publicly defended insurance mogul Hank Greenburg. According to Whitehead, Spitzer said "You will pay dearly for what you have done. You will wish you had never written that letter."

Since taking over as New York's chief executive, Spitzer's name-calling, swearing and temper tantrums have frequently made front-page headlines. When Assemblyman Tedisco dared to question a Spitzer proposal, the governor described himself as a "f***ing steamroller" who would flatten anyone in his way. He told Orange County Senator William Larkin he'd "cut [his] head off." And when Senate Republican Majority Leader Joe Bruno recommended a grand jury investigation into allegations that the state police was used to spy on him, Spitzer called the 78-year old Bruno "an old senile piece of s*** who is under federal investigation."

Miffed because the state legislature doesn't bow to his commands, Spitzer recently proclaimed he just won't deal with them anymore. "There is an unbelievable opportunity now," he said, "to govern through the agencies, and that's frankly what I'm really looking forward to."

Spitzer is taking a page from the playbook of his famous predecessor, Governor Nelson Rockefeller, who led the pack in finding ways to get around voter disapproval of spending schemes. Rockefeller created a shadow government in the form of authorities and agencies that spent billions outside the state budget and without the approval or control of either the legislature or the voters. Now Governor Spitzer, who promised a transparent government, is retreating to these big-government murky mazes to impose his will on the populace.

Spitzer's "no-holds-barred" approach to governing has been adopted by his staffers. These "best and the brightest" believe that bare-knuckle tactics are permissible against perceived Albany obstructionists who in their judgment are dumb, wrong or evil. This brazen attitude has given rise to abuse of power scandals that are wrecking the seven-month old administration.

In April, the governor's Deputy Secretary for Energy, Steven Mitnick, was accused of threatening a New York State Public Service Commissioner over a policy disagreement. With the expected release of a critical Inspector General's report, Mitnick resigned his post on Friday, August 4, 2007.

In July, State Attorney General Andrew Cuomo released a blockbuster report detailing the governor's top aides misuse of the state police when attempting to destroy Senator Bruno with manufactured documents claiming he broke state law.

Although the governor denied any knowledge of the plot, claimed his office cooperated with investigators, punished the culprits, and in a *New York Times* op-ed apologized for violations of his pledge "to maintain the highest ethical standards," Albany pundits do not believe Spitzer is in the clear.

Doubts of Spitzer's innocence increased when it was revealed that the governor's Chief of Staff Richard Baum and one of the conspirators, suspended Communications Director Darren Dopp, refused to be interviewed by the Attorney General's office. (The A.G. does not have subpoena power, hence they could not be compelled to testify.)

For weeks Spitzer has been stonewalling the press, refusing to explain why he did not direct his aides to testify, and giving dubious legalistic rationales as to why special prosecutors and senate investigators should not be empanelled to subpoena the governor and his aides.

Few, however, are buying the Spitzer tap dance. *The New York Post*'s Fred Dicker has described Troopergate as "a ten in terms of Albany scandals" and says it is "the biggest political scandal in modern New York history involving the governor and his office."

New York Daily News liberal columnist Michael Goodwin called for a grand jury investigation and bluntly stated: "I believe Eliot Spitzer not only knew about the scheme, I believe he approved it and maybe even ordered it."

Eliot Spitzer's woes are far from over. On August 1, 2007, Albany County District Attorney David Soares ordered a criminal investigation into Troopergate. And his administration is expected to be paralyzed for months answering subpoenas from up to four separate inquiries into the misconduct charges.

In 2005, when discussing his soccer playing days, Spitzer made this revealing comment: "You play hard, you play rough, and hopefully you don't get caught." Governor Spitzer has certainly played hard and rough politics but like the "best and the brightest" of the 1960s, he too might be caught up in a quagmire from which there is no escape.

August 18, 2007

Governor Spitzer's *Summa Theologica*

Theologian Reinhold Niebuhr, hero of post-World War II "vital center" liberals, must be rolling in his grave.

At the Chautauqua Institution on August 7, New York's politically wounded governor, Eliot Spitzer, in a speech titled "The Need for Both Passion and Humility in Politics," invoked Niebuhr to knock President Bush's Iraq policy and excuse Spitzer's administration's unethical conduct.

The governor, whose previous theological speculation was pretty much limited to describing himself as a "f***ing steamroller," now says that we "need a sense of modesty about the virtue, wisdom and power available to us" and "a sense of contrition about the human frailties and foibles which lie at the foundation of both the enemy's demonry and our vanities."

New York's enemy is the status quo which "drives the injustices of our time." The status quo, says the governor, "simply represents the policies I oppose."

To "realize a Progressive Era for the 21st Century" and to achieve what is morally right, Spitzer acknowledges that Niebuhr's principles of humility were abandoned: "We were fighting so hard for what we believed was right that we let down our guard and allowed our passion to get the best of us."

Spitzer's public confession is flawed. He does not understand that the "Progressive Era" he seeks to realize already exists. The "status quo" he despises is actually the product of a half century of progressive policies. New York's progressives created the politics of control and coercion that is destroying the Empire State. They have been the guardians of the forces responsible for the sorry plight of New York's educational and health care systems and its physical infrastructure.

The Progressives sanctioned Albany's fiscal mismanagement, spending sprees and excessive taxes.

The Progressives absconded with capital projects monies

to fund bloated general operating budgets, thus causing the neglect and decay of New York's infrastructure.

The Progressives created New York's $44 billion Medicaid program that cuddles the Health Care cartel and is bankruping county governments throughout the State.

The Progressives pumped billions into failing inner-city public schools to pacify the teachers union.

And since taking office, Governor Spitzer has rolled in the mud with these status quo Progressives:

- Spitzer capitulated on the Campaign for Fiscal Equity Suit and poured billions of additional state tax dollars into New York City's abysmally inefficient school system.
- Spitzer agreed to a state spending increase of 9 percent – three times the inflation rate – approved $300 million in legislative pork, and supports pay raises for part-time legislators.
- Spitzer enhanced the power of status quo state and municipal unions by signing an executive order that grants 60,000 child care workers the right to unionize.
- Spitzer exempted state and municipal union political action committees from campaign reform restrictions.

And Spitzer's Chautauqua speech claim that he enacted the largest property tax cut in state history is a lie. The School Tax Relief Program (STAR) is not a tax-cutting program but an income redistribution plan – a sort of homestead exemption. The state subsidizes homeowners with a yearly relief check while school districts continue to tax and spend without restraint.

Eliot Spitzer is not an agent for change; he is just another progressive enabler.

As for Spitzer's public mea culpa for his aides' misdeeds – publicly accepting responsibility for these actions is not enough. To be a true penitent, there must be the admission of all wrongdoings; nothing can be withheld. The governor must stop the stonewalling and permit a proper and thorough investigation of Troopergate.

Governor Spitzer is mistaken if he thinks his Chautauqua theological musings put his administration's scandals behind him. His pledge to "give scrutiny to the rightness of our means" has only increased demands that he come clean.

January 13, 2008

Spitzer in Wonderland: The 2008 State of the State Address

New York State is on the edge of an economic abyss. Citibank, which will write off about $18 billion, has announced it will lay off over 30,000 employees – most of whom work in New York. Merrill Lynch, anticipating losses to top $15 billion, is turning to China and the Middle East to raise the capital needed to survive. In 2007, over 40,000 people in the securities industry were fired, bonus payouts were significantly reduced, and more of the same is expected in 2008.

With twenty percent of the state's tax revenues coming from Wall Street-related enterprises one would think this spells big trouble for New York. But these economic woes did not appear to faze Governor Spitzer when he delivered his State of the State address last week.

Instead of announcing "the days of wine and roses" are over, instead of declaring a fiscal state of emergency, instead of calling for across-the-board spending cuts and a hiring freeze, Spitzer proposed increases in state spending.

The governor's speech, which reads like a dry brief composed by a committee of pedantic lawyers, is devoid of reality. Let's review the key components:

A. Last year Governor Spitzer lied when he called the expanded School Tax Relief Program (STAR) the largest tax cut in the state's history. STAR does not cut or cap school district property taxes. In 1997, Governor Pataki dropped the key component of the proposed program – school district tax increases limited to 4 percent or the regional consumer price index, whichever is lower – to get it through the legislature. As a result, STAR merely redistributes income. The state takes money from one taxpayer and gives it to another.

In his State of the State address, Spitzer employed political newspeak: He dropped the "largest tax cut" claim and redefined STAR as a "rebate" program. But instead of demanding that the legislature add a tax cap feature to the 2008 STAR program, he took the coward's way out and announced the creation of a commission that will investigate tax relief alternatives.

The governor stuck his former primary opponent, Tom Suozzi, with the thankless task of chairing the bipartisan commission. Suozzi, not Spitzer, will have to take the heat from the big government interest groups (i.e., the teachers union). Expect Suozzi to issue an illusionary tax relief report that masks cap exceptions with flowery rhetoric.

B. To fund increased spending on the State University System, Spitzer calls for "unlock[ing] some of the value of the New York lottery." In other words, the governor wants to borrow billions collateralized with gambling revenues.

Since most lottery tickets are purchased by senior citizens on fixed income and poor people, Spitzer's spending program depends on exploiting the gambling habits of these downtrodden folks. What a cynical plan. No wonder the Manhattan Institute's E.J. McMahon calls it the "motherload of one shots."

C. Governor Spitzer wants to spend $1 billion to revitalize upstate New York. He believes that increased government spending "for investing in business, in infrastructure needed to create shovel-ready sites and in agribusiness" will turn the tide in the economically depressed region.

Spitzer, like his predecessor George Pataki, fails to grasp that until upstate's inequitable property tax levies are reduced, huge infusions of state dollars will have little impact. Albany's unfunded state mandates, which consume up to 80 percent of property tax revenues in many counties, must be eliminated if that region is to be economically viable.

D. Spitzer also wants to spend more on education, health care for children, housing and infrastructure. And he believes all these programs can be funded without raising taxes.

The United States is in a recession. It is likely that New York will be hit harder and take longer to recover from the economic downturn than the rest of the nation.

Governor Spitzer must adjust his budget to cope with this reality. If he does not, his only alternative will be to raise taxes to finance his spending schemes. If that happens, expect even greater job losses and the accompanying decline in population and tax revenues.

March 25, 2008

Governor David Paterson of New York: Super Liberal

Since David Paterson was sworn in as New York's 55th governor to replace the disgraced Eliot Spitzer, the media has focused on his sexual escapades and his use of campaign contributions to fund non-political expenses. There is, however, more to Paterson than bad soap opera: throughout his government career he has enthusiastically embraced the fiscal, economic and cultural agenda of the radical left.

Before his election to the office of lieutenant governor in November 2006, State Senator Paterson represented for twenty years the Manhattan neighborhood of Harlem. During his tenure, Senator Paterson's New York Conservative Party legislative rating average was approximately 36 percent.

Paterson consistently supported the tax, borrow and spend policies of governors Mario Cuomo and George Pataki. He voted for the tax and fee increases that caused New York to have the nation's highest income tax burden, state and local taxes per capita and debt per capita. In 2003, for instance, Paterson voted for the Omnibus Budget Bill which included the largest tax increase in the history of New York State.

Paterson opposed numerous proposals that would have established constitutional spending caps, limitations on state spending, reform measures that would require voter approval of all state-supported bonded debt, and state construction spending caps.

One measure he always voted to extend – New York's antiquated rent control laws. In 1992, he even voted against the elimination of rent control on luxury apartments.

As for social issues, Paterson proudly led the charge for left-wing cultural causes.

He voted for the state "Gay Rights" and "Bias Crime" bills. He voted to end the "conscience clause" for religious institutions which forces Catholic education and medical institutions to provide services contrary to religious principles.

Paterson supported funding of abortion and partial birth abortion, and opposed parental consent for teenage abortions.

He voted against bills that would have permitted HIV testing of newborns and increased penalties for child pornography criminals.

In 1995, he opposed excluding illegal aliens from receiving welfare and in 1996, he voted nay on legislation that would have excluded illegals from receiving publicly funded health care.

And contrary to some reports Paterson does not support vouchers or charter schools. He voted against the 1999 bill that enacted the "New York Charter School Act of 1998" and established the charter school stimulus fund.

Paterson is also very tight with New York's Working Families Party which the Manhattan Institute's Sol Stein describes as promoters of "1960s bred agenda of anti-capitalism, central planning, victimology and government handouts to the poor."

Unlike his elitist predecessor, David Paterson is an affable person who likes hanging out in Albany pubs swapping stories and downing cocktails with political cronies. He has been a "get along" guy who has advanced his career by supporting the policies that have destroyed the once mighty Empire State. Expect the Paterson administration to continue the Albany tradition of fiscal sleight-of-hand to convince the public that the state budget is "responsibly" balanced – all the while pandering to special interests and increasing spending, taxes and pork.

February 4, 2010

Paterson Doctrine: Judge What I Say, Not What I Do

When Gov. David Paterson completed his Jan. 6 State of the State address, reporters proceeded to do what they always do, run around the Assembly chamber asking political heavies for their reaction to the speech.

This year the most obvious person to ask was Attorney General Andrew Cuomo. The A.G. gave an even-handed response. He acknowledged that the governor articulated the state's problems, and then said, "The key now, however, is to get it done. To solve these problems in these times will require sustained effort, seriousness of purpose and the ability to build a coalition for change."

The next morning, on a talk radio show, the governor gave this reaction to Cuomo's call for action: "One of the problems, I think in government and State of the State addresses is there's a scorecard. We measure the person by how much they pass as opposed to how much is right." In other words, the governor wants to be judged not by what he does but what he says.

What a bizarre comment. Apparently the governor has forgotten the maxim we were taught in grammar school, "Actions speak louder than words."

Philosophers throughout history have called on people to act on their principles. Aristotle declared in "Politics," "Felicity is a state of activity; and it is the actions of just and temperate men which are the fulfillment of a great part of goodness."

Franklin Delano Roosevelt, at the 1932 Democratic convention, not only described New Deal principles to tackle the Great Depression, but in a booming voice told his listeners that the situation "calls for action and action now." And F.D.R. acted.

Winston Churchill reminded the British people during the Blitz that "there is great hope provided action is taken worthy of the opportunity."

These men knew that delivering speeches was not enough

to meet the challenges of their day. Roosevelt and Churchill knew history would judge them by the consequences of their actions.

There may, however, be some method to the governor's maddening doctrine. He may want to be judged merely by his rhetoric or intentions because his pubic achievements have been few in number.

Throughout his 20 years in the state Senate, Paterson spent most of his time talking in Albany bistros, saloons, discothèques and New Jersey steakhouses. In the Senate chamber, he was not a mover and shaker, and routinely voted for increased spending and taxes.

Since assuming the office of governor, Paterson has given plenty of speeches, told lots of jokes and issued countless press releases. However, following through on his public policy pronouncements has not been his strong suit. Here are a few examples:

In January 2009, he pledged to cut state spending, downsize the bloated government labor force and not to increase taxes. Four months later he approved a budget that increased spending 10 percent (five times the inflation rate), raised the state income tax and included no layoffs.

Every time he called the Legislature into special session to address the state's growing budget deficit, he failed to enact his proposed cuts. Nothing happened. The bored legislators dismissed the governor's threats and went home.

For the 2010–2011 state budget year, Paterson has claimed he has courageously and prudently addressed the $7.3 billion revenue shortfall by slashing spending. In fact, the proposed budget increases spending by $2 billion and utilizes a score of imprudent fiscal gimmicks, including one-shot revenue, tax and fee increases.

David Paterson is no profile in courage. He does not possess the grit necessary to be a man of action like FDR or Churchill.

The only time I will celebrate the "judge what I say" Paterson doctrine is when he says these words: "I will not seek a full term as governor of New York." For our beleaguered state that day can't come soon enough.

August 13, 2010

Political Corruption, Served Up NY Style

As New York sinks further into the fiscal abyss, shameless members of our political class are out of control in their quests to sidestep the law, line their pockets or enrich their families and cronies.

On the federal level, let's start with the dean of New York's congressional delegation, U.S. Rep. Charles Rangel. The 20-term representative has been charged with failing to disclose $1.7 million of personal assets; failing to pay taxes on $75,000 in rental income; receiving improper benefits from the use of four rent-stabilized apartments; and using office stationery to solicit funds for a charity named after him.

Then there's U.S. Rep. Gary Ackerman who, after making a $100,000 profit on Xenonics Inc., held a meeting in his congressional office with Xenonics employees and representatives of the Israeli government. His actions appear to violate House ethic rules.

He's followed by U.S. Rep. Gregory Meeks, who is being investigated by the feds over a charity scandal and confessed to failing to report $55,000 in personal loans. (In 1985, Idaho Congressman George Hansen served time for not disclosing loans made to him.)

As for this year's Albany scandals, here's a sampling:

- Gov. David Paterson is being investigated to determine if he lied about receiving Yankee tickets worth $2,000, and if there was a quid pro quo for awarding the Aqueduct racing contract to a politically connected consortium.
- Senate Majority Leader Pedro Espada Jr. was accused in a civil suit filed by A.G. Andrew Cuomo of diverting over $14 million from nonprofit clinics he founded. The U.S. attorney is heading a criminal investigation.
- The Senate's Temporary President Malcolm Smith is being investigated by the U.S. attorney concerning $111,000 in

members' items that were being steered to New Directions Development Corp. of Queens.

- Senate Democratic Conference Leader John Sampson did legal work for a shady Queens real estate broker being investigated for fraud and predatory lending.
- State Sen. Hiram Monserrate was expelled by his colleagues after being convicted of assaulting a lady friend.
- Former state Sen. Efrain Gonzalez Jr. was sentenced to seven years for stealing hundreds of thousands from nonprofit groups.

Reacting to these scandals, Cuomo put it this way: "The amount of political dysfunction in Albany is matched only by the lack of integrity."

Local governments are not exempt from corruption charges: New York City Councilman Larry Seabrook was hit with a 13-count federal indictment involving $1.2 million of city money granted to nonprofits controlled by his brother and two sisters.

And in Nassau, two former county legislators, Roger Corbin and Patrick Williams, and two North Hempstead officials, Neville Mullings and David Wasserman, were indicted by the D.A. on charges of theft, conspiracy and fraud in connection with the New Cassel Redevelopment Project.

Political parties are also in the muck: The Working Families Party, a creation of ACORN and public employee unions, is being investigated by the U.S. attorney over campaign finance activities.

Manhattan's D.A. indicted Republican John Haggerty in June for allegedly gleaning $750,000 from the Independence Party. Party Chairman Frank McKay is under investigation by two district attorneys for roles he played in 2009 New York City races. Political wags are also wondering if it was a coincidence that both 2006 Republican A.G. candidate Jeanine Pirro and 2010 GOP Comptroller candidate Harry Wilson hired the Roosevelt Group, a mysterious political consulting firm with ties to the party, after receiving their respective Independence Party nominations.

Corruption in New York has reached epidemic proportions because too many pols are vain, arrogant people who believe that their lofty positions place them above the rules. Holding office is not about principles or the pursuit of the common good, but about the spoils of office: lifestyle, patronage, contracts, favors, deals and money.

Our state is in fiscal crisis and while many wonder whether the state's best days may be behind it, this "damn the taxpayer" behavior is turning the once-mighty Empire State into a municipal desert.

June 4, 2010

NY Mandates Strangle Local Governments

In a recent meeting held to discuss suburban problems, the county executives of Nassau, Suffolk and Westchester agreed that unfunded state mandates are consuming too big a share of their budgets. Nassau's Ed Mangano, speaking for the group, said, "None of us can afford one more unfunded mandate. We want to make that clear."

For years governors and state legislators have been evading the responsibility of funding programs they wanted by ordering municipalities and school districts to provide and pay for a host of services. To comply with these unfunded mandates, local governments are forced to raise billions in taxes. This, in part, explains why New York's local per capita taxes are the highest in the nation.

Studies have revealed that New York imposes more mandates than any other state - over 2,000. These mandates consume on average 60 percent of county government budgets.

The Citizens Budget Commission has explained that the main reason for the crippling level of taxation is state policies on Medicaid, education and collective bargaining between unions and local governments.

The Manhattan Institute's E.J. McMahon agreed: "What this underscores is that the problem we have is a four-letter word: cost. The costs are driven primarily out of Albany, by the state legislature and the governor. But though the costs are dictated by Albany, Albany does not have to foot the whole bill; that's the main problem. All they do in Albany is cash the campaign contributions from all the interest groups that benefit from their spending, primarily the unions."

Medicaid is the poster child for unfunded mandates. Created during the "Great Society" heyday, Title 19 of the Social Security Act of 1965 established guidelines for a Medicaid program that states could adopt to provide medical services for the poor. The federal government would cover half the cost and the states would have to pay the other half.

New York quickly signed on to the program, added numerous amendments that made dependency a way of life and decreed that Albany would pick up only half the state's portion of Medicaid costs; the rest of the financial burden would have to be shouldered by local governments. As a result, today the average New York county devotes about half of its property taxes to covering its imposed share of Medicaid costs. In Nassau County, the local share of Medicaid is nearly $250 million annually, in Suffolk $230 million - roughly 30 percent of their property tax collections.

The other cause of local government's skyrocketing cost: New York's public sector labor laws.

With employee salaries and benefits accounting for about 75 percent of municipal and school district operating expenses, possessing the power to effectively negotiate fair contracts is essential. Unfortunately this is not the case in New York. Over the years the state legislature, succumbing to the demands of public employee unions, has enacted legislation that puts municipal employers at a disadvantage at the bargaining table.

Here are a few examples: The Public Employee Relations Board hinders municipal employers from implementing cost-saving policies such as subcontracting of services. The Triborough Amendment forbids employers from altering "terms and conditions of employment" after a contract has expired. As a result, teacher unions, for example, have no incentive to seriously negotiate since their members are guaranteed pay increases even in the absence of a contract.

These and scores of other laws, rules and regulations that favor municipal unions explain why the average salary of government workers is higher than private sector employees and why government benefits exceed those in the private sector.

Because time after time Albany's "powers that be" have, for short-term political advantage, forced mandates without regard to potential consequences, New York's local governments and school districts are on the edge of a fiscal abyss.

December 10, 2008

Slouching towards Insolvency – and Servitude

During America's recent economic boom, state governments were on a huge spending spree. Believing they knew better than local municipal leaders and anxious to buy the loyalty of special interest groups, many state leaders lavishly funded every hare-brained program – particularly in the field of education and health care. While initiatives of this kind may sometimes reflect Catholic social principles, staying solvent should be part of the authentic virtue of solidarity, because bankruptcy has both a financial and moral cost.

Since 2003, total spending of the 50 states increased annually by 6.4 percent (more than twice the inflation rate), their total outstanding debt, about $2.19 trillion, increased a whopping 38 percent, and their collective operating deficit is expected to hit $140 billion.

In the aftermath of the Wall Street meltdown, with their tax revenues declining and rainy day funds depleted – instead of warning that fiscal restraint is required because the days of wine and roses are over – many weak, cowardly state leaders are demanding that they be rewarded for failure and receive federal bailout money in order to continue funding their fiscal follies.

It wasn't always like this. In fact state constitutions were specifically designed to maintain fiscal integrity by giving local municipalities and their citizen-taxpayers the maximum authority to make fiscal and policy decisions. The authors of state constitutions instinctively practiced subsidiarity (long championed in Catholic social thought) which, to quote Michael Novak, "maintains human life proceeds most intelligently and creatively when decisions are made at the local level closest to concrete reality."

This approach to governing led to the creation of over 80,000 municipalities nationally – counties, cities, towns, villages, hamlets – that successfully provided essential public safety services and the building and maintenance of schools and libraries, fire, water, and electrical facilities, roads and bridges. Since the New Deal days, however, federal and state magistrates have been destroying local governing by imposing unfunded mandates, regional consolidations, and financial aid with ideological strings attached. And my home state of New York has been the model for these big-government types.

In the post-World War II era, New York, with over 2,600 municipal subdivisions, was truly the Empire State, indeed the leading industrial state in the nation, with a population of 16.7 million and the largest block of electoral votes at forty-five. Its major cities – New York, Buffalo, Rochester, Syracuse, Utica, Binghamton, and Schenectady – were thriving. Sixty years later, New York's state government is dysfunctional, its financial coffers empty, its industrial base destroyed, and its fleeing upstate population (1.5 million have moved out since 2000) is turning many cities into municipal deserts. Down to twenty-nine electoral votes, New York's national influence is ever smaller.

Buffalo, for example, once the largest flour-mill city in the western world and America's fourth largest manufacturing city, is now on the edge of bankruptcy. It has lost 48 percent of its population since 1960, lost its heavy industry and manufacturing base, and has 35,000 abandoned single-family homes. In 2006, Buffalo's mayor even called for the dissolution of his city.

Why the decline? Big-spending New York governors from Nelson Rockefeller to David Paterson circumvented taxpayer oversight and neutered local governments by employing fiscal gimmicks that concealed deficit spending, created hundreds of government agencies that have independent spending power, increased layers of bureaucratic oversight, and imposed unfunded state mandates.

Rockefeller, whose 15-year reign stretched from 1959 to 1973, earned the distinction of having imposed more tax increases – fully 18 – than any governor in state history. Rocky created a massive state bureaucracy including 230 government agencies and issued $12 billion in debt.

During the governorships of Mario Cuomo (1983–1994) and George Pataki (1995–2006) total state funds spending grew from $20.9 billion to $80 billion – twice the inflation rate. Debt during the period jumped from $20 billion to $51 billion.

The most destructive fiscal gimmick employed by the state government to impose their will on local municipalities – unfunded mandates. The CEO of the Rochester Business Alliance recently declared, "Upstate [New York] is absolutely sinking under these mandates."

The mega-unfunded mandate is the very liberal Medicaid program. Hatched by Rockefeller and expanded by his successors, today the program costs more than the combined Medicaid expenditures of America's two largest states – California and Texas.

The average New York county devotes more than 60 percent of its taxes to cover its state-imposed share of Medicaid costs. An Erie County official told *The New York Times* that "Every penny we take in county property taxes is used to pay for Medicaid. This is before we pay for any libraries or plow any roads or pay any police services."

After years of uncontrolled spending, New York has the highest local taxes, the highest combined state and local taxes in the country, and a projected three-year deficit totaling $46 billion. As a result, jobs have disappeared at an alarming rate and manufacturers have moved to the south, Europe, and India. Buffalo, Syracuse, Rochester, and Schenectady – onetime centers of commerce, industry, and technology – are facing financial and economic doom.

The big-government crowd that dominates Albany and many other state capitals are intent on destroying local governments, no matter what the financial cost, because they reject the fundamental democratic premise that people should be relied on primarily to govern themselves. Andrew Greeley has postulated that these elites despise local governments because they "are not modern and what is not modern is conservative, reactionary, unprogressive, unenlightened, superstitious, and just plain wrong."

Expect the community organizers taking over Washington in January to agree to bail out the states so they can continue their mission to destroy the autonomy of America's cities and citizens.

August 7, 2009

George Pataki: A Man for the Silly Season

British journalist G.K. Chesterton described this time of year when politicians grope to get the attention of the general public occupied with important matters (i.e., vacationing with their families, preparing their children's return to school) as the "Silly Season."

One pol who comes out of the woodwork every Silly Season is the attention-starved former governor of New York, George Pataki.

Last year at this time, Pataki, who attended the National Republican Convention as a spectator, not a delegate, told the New York delegation, "I'm back! I'm getting involved."

My reaction to his declaration: Back to do what? To further destroy New York's economy? To further decimate New York's Republican Party? To further corrupt New York's body politic?

Several weeks later when asked if the "current delays at the World Trade Center came as a result of mistakes in his administration," George Pataki gave this incredible answer: "That's utter nonsense!"

Frankly, his attempt at historic revisionism was utter nonsense!

In the aftermath of the 9/11 tragedy, George Pataki bet his gubernatorial legacy on the rebuilding of Ground Zero and lost. Five years of mishaps on his watch proved the ineptitude of an administration. If Pataki had stood by the belief he expressed in his first term - that government should not be in the commercial real estate business - lower Manhattan would not be referred to today as "Pataki's Pit."

Viewing the mess at the end of the Pataki administration, columnist John Podhoretz declared: "Through a poisonous combination of arrogance, indolence, cowardice and foolishness, Pataki has made sure that the crater created by al Qaeda will remain unfilled for at least nine years. . . . Pataki didn't bother to get it right. He didn't bother much at all. His carelessness with this world historical matter makes him unfit to serve even one more day as governor."

In this year's Silly Season media foray, Pataki said in late July he plans on continuing to play a role in politics, has not ruled out running for office, and will make his decision public in 2010.

It appears that Pataki still doesn't grasp that the day he left office he fell off New York's radar screen. While Hugh Carey is revered to this day and Mario Cuomo is politically relevant, Pataki is a forgotten man.

New Yorkers have consigned Pataki to oblivion because during his three terms in office he discarded his political philosophy to retain power and perks. As *New York Post* editor Robert McManus observed, "Policy play[ed] second fiddle to perception and expedience."

Pataki abandoned his pledges to curb Medicare costs, unfunded state mandates, one-shot fiscal gimmicks, back-door borrowing and tax and fee increases.

As a result of Pataki's insouciant leadership, when he left office in 2006, New York had the highest state and local tax burden, highest state taxes per capita, worst business tax climate, and New York was rated the worst in the U.S. Economic Freedom Index in the nation.

The New York Observer summed up the Pataki years as "a legacy of laziness, mediocrity and pervasive neglect of the public interest, while creating a culture in which ethical corruption has become an acceptable way of life."

And that legacy haunts us to this day. Take the mess at the MTA. Rather than take advantage of boom times to prepare the transit system for the future, Pataki deferred critical investment and avoided confronting out of control union costs. Due to Pataki's failures, MTA annual debt service increased 50 percent in the last five years and is due to exceed $2 billion by 2012. This occurred because Pataki in effect borrowed for operating costs and refunded existing debt over 30 years in order to delay fare increases.

It is inconceivable that Pataki believes New Yorkers will welcome him back to public life with open arms. One can only assume that Pataki's annual Silly Season "I'm back" pronouncement is to promote his low-profile business interests.

April 16, 2007

Rudy Giuliani: Lifelong Liberal

Former New York City mayor Rudy Giuliani has been barn-storming the nation, claiming the Ronald Reagan mantle. Recent opinion polls suggest his campaign is striking a chord with the GOP's rank and file but indicate most Republicans don't really know where Mr. Giuliani stands on key issues.

Those who do know are glossing over some very striking philosophical flaws – at least from a truly conservative perspective. Rudy not only supports abortion but also has advocated for partial-birth abortion and government funding of abortion. He favors gun control, gay rights, domestic partnerships and bias-crime laws. And that's just a short list.

As a conservative activist who has observed Giuliani for many years (and who ran against him in the 1993 mayoral election), I can say categorically that he is not now, nor has he ever been, a conservative. In my judgment, his record leaves no doubt that he's a lifelong liberal.

In college, Rudy attacked senator Barry Goldwater of Arizona, the 1964 GOP presidential nominee, as an "incompetent, confused and sometimes idiotic man," and he urged Republicans to "find men who will adequately address themselves to the problems of discrimination, of poverty, of education, of public housing and the many more problems that Sen. Goldwater and company throw aside in the name of small laissez-faire government."

Former New York governor Mario Cuomo, a liberal icon, put it this way: "(Giuliani's) basically very pragmatic. And he's progressive. He is not a Neanderthal, a primitive conservative. But look, he's a clever human being. He can shave and draw fine distinctions when he needs to."

Giuliani's first wife, Regina, agreed. She told Giuliani biographer Wayne Barrett that when she and Rudy separated in 1980, she "still considered him to be a liberal Democrat." She also observed that "(Rudy) generally won't do things unless he believes them, ... but he's not a saint, and he will do things that serve his interests."

Rudy first switched from Democrat to Independent, and then to Republican, not because he embraced the tenets of conservatism but in order to move up the U.S. Justice Department ladder.

"He only became a Republican after he began to get all these (Justice Department) jobs," Rudy's mother, Helen Giuliani, told Barrett. "He's definitely not a conservative Republican. He thinks he is, but he isn't. He still feels very sorry for the poor."

As a candidate for mayor of New York, Giuliani distanced himself from Ronald Reagan and the GOP. During his first mayoral bid, in 1989, *The New York Times* pointed out that he "noted frequently that he was supported by the liberal wing of the Republican Party and maintained that he never embraced Mr. Reagan's broad conservative agenda." And when conservatives attacked him during that 1993 mayoral campaign, Giuliani said, "Their fear of me is that I'm going to be a beachhead for the establishment of a more progressive form of Republicanism."

On another occasion he told a television host, "I do not look to see what the catechism of conservatism says about how to solve a problem."

And we mustn't forget that when Giuliani endorsed governor Cuomo for reelection to a fourth term in 1994, he did so, he said, because Republican George Pataki had "a very right-wing voting record" and because Pataki proposed an "irresponsible" 25 percent state income tax cut.

Giuliani also seriously considered endorsing Bill Clinton in 1996 and instead backed Republican nominee Bob Dole with very little fanfare.

"Most of Clinton's policies," he said at the time, "are very similar to mine."

Some Republicans and conservatives are now claiming that Rudy has changed and really become more conservative, and they cite as an example his abandonment of his former vehement opposition to school vouchers. But when Rudy Crew, former New York City Public Schools chancellor, asked Giuliani about this policy shift, the mayor said, "Don't worry about it. It's just a political thing, a campaign thing. I'm not going to do anything. Don't take it seriously." This particular rightward shift was simply a ploy to enhance Giuliani's 2000 U.S. Senate candidacy.

Contrary to what we've been hearing and reading, Rudy Giuliani is today what he has always been: a liberal. Conservatives should take stories of his Damascus Road-like conversion with a grain of salt. Rudy, like Hillary, is campaigning for the presidency in order to implement lifelong leftist beliefs.

April 4, 2007

Rudy Giuliani, NO Fiscal Conservative

When Steve Forbes was seeking the Republican presidential nomination in 1996, then-Mayor Rudy Giuliani ridiculed his proposal to scrap the federal income tax code and replace it with a simple flat-tax. Giuliani called Forbes plan a "mistake" and said if implemented, it "would really be a disaster."

Despite these smears, Steve Forbes now believes Rudy embraces the flat-tax concept and endorsed him for president, claiming he "will inspire the next generation of the Reagan Revolution."

Apparently Forbes forgot that when running for mayor, Rudy Giuliani showcased his liberal credentials and boasted he would "rekindle the Rockefeller, Javits Lefkowitz tradition" of the Republican Party and "produce the kind of change New York City saw with Fiorella LaGuardia and with John Lindsay."

Here's a sampling of the change the Rockefeller-Lindsay brand of Republican liberalism gave New York: During Governor Rockefeller's 14-year tenure, he brought New York State to the verge of bankruptcy. When Rocky entered office, his first budget was $2 billion, when he left office his last budget was $8.7 billion. Thanks to 18 tax increases he signed into law, New Yorkers were the most heavily taxed citizens in the nation and their state had the highest public debt in the nation. Viewing the mess he inherited from Rockefeller, Democratic Governor Hugh Carey said: "I've seen delicatessens in bankruptcy in better shape than the State of New York."

The Upper East Side Republican-liberal social engineer mayor, John Lindsay, financed New York City's big government agenda with creative fiscal gimmicks including phantom revenues, capitalization of expenses, short-term debt rollovers, false revenue estimates and excessive long-term borrowing. And Lindsay increased nuisance taxes, water rates, sewer taxes and commercial rent tax, and instituted the city's personal income, general corporation and unincorporated business taxes.

Mayor Lindsay's reckless fiscal policies were directly responsible for the City's 1975 default on debt.

Following in their footsteps, Mayor Giuliani declared that pledging no new tax increases is "political pandering." He also said, "when I ran for mayor both times, I was asked very, very often to do the following: Pledge that you will never raise taxes. I refused to do that. Pledge that you will lower taxes. I refused to do that."

When Giuliani endorsed liberal icon Mario Cuomo for governor in 1994, he called the Republican-Conservative George Pataki's 25 percent state income tax cut (cloned from the Forbes-inspired New Jersey income tax cut) "irresponsible" and a "shell game that would hurt everyone in the state."

Forbes points to Rudy's fiscal management of New York City as proof of his conservatism. "Giuliani," he claims, "turned an inherited deficit [$2.3 billion] into a multimillion dollar surplus." It's true that during Giuliani's first term when times were tough, he contained costs and made some tax cuts. But what Forbes failed to point out is that in Rudy's second term, when the economy was booming, he abandoned fiscal restraint and became a big-spending liberal. City budget expenditures jumped 25 percent – twice the inflation rate – and Giuliani left his successor a projected operating deficit of $4.5 billion and New York's citizens with the highest tax burden in any major municipality in America.

Rudy Giuliani, a legatee of Nelson Rockefeller and John Lindsay, fails on every fiscal and cultural issue that is dear to conservatives. And one can only hope that Steve Forbes and his friends will learn before it's too late that life-long liberal Rudy Giuliani is employing conservative rhetoric merely to patronize them.

November 19, 2007

Giuliani's Catholic Problem Won't Go Away

A 2008 voter's guide created by Catholic bishops no doubt has Giuliani supporters scrambling for loopholes that can be used to convince Catholics that it's okay to vote for Rudy Giuliani despite his pro-abortion stand.

At the conclusion of their national conference held in Baltimore, the American Catholic Bishops announced they adopted "Forming Consciences for Faithful Citizenship," a statement of principles to guide Catholic voters in the 2008 presidential election.

The Bishops' guide affirms the Vatican's *"Worthiness to Receive Holy Communion – General Principles,"* written by then-Cardinal Joseph Ratzinger in 2004.

In that statement, Ratzinger pulled the rug out from under the proponents of the "seamless garment" argument by making it perfectly clear that not all moral issues have the same moral weight as abortion and euthanasia.

"There may be," he declared, "a legitimate diversity of opinion even among Catholics about waging war and applying the death penalty, but not, however, with regard to abortion and euthanasia." When it comes to abortion, death penalty, or the war in Iraq, only abortion is intrinsically wrong because it destroys innocent human life.

On the death penalty and the war, Ratzinger confirmed that the Church does not hold a univocal view.

While it is true that Pope John Paul II and the U.S. bishops oppose the death penalty, they have never decried the Church's stand on capital punishment. In fact, in a 1980 pastoral letter, the American Bishops insisted that "the state has the right to take the life of a person guilty of a serious crime."

Catholics are free to oppose using the death penalty in particular situations, but Catholics are not free to condemn it in the name of the Church as always morally wrong.

Likewise, while the Vatican opposed the U.S. invasion of

Iraq, Catholics were free to use prudential judgment in determining if it was just. The U.S. Conference of Catholic Bishops stressed that "reasonable people can disagree about the necessity of using force" to overthrow Saddam.

In 2004, Catholic Kerry supporters jumped on Ratzinger's last paragraph to rationalize their support for the pro-abortion presidential candidate: "When a Catholic does not share a candidate's stand in favour of abortion and/or euthanasia, but votes for that candidate for other reasons, it is considered remote material cooperation, which can be permitted in the presence of proportionate reasons."

The Rev. Andrew Greeley led the way, declaring that Catholics could, in good conscience, vote for Kerry because the right-wing Ratzinger said so.

In his nationally syndicated column, Greeley quoted that final paragraph and concluded: "It is as close to an official statement on the subject as one is likely to get. It says that Catholics are not obliged to vote on one issue, no matter how important the issue might be. They may vote for Kerry 'for other reasons' so long as they are not supporting him merely for his pro-choice stance. This ought to settle the matter."

Quoting only one paragraph of the statement and not properly explaining the phrase "proportionate reasoning" allowed Greeley to mislead his readers.

Dr. Robert Royal, president of the Washington-based Faith and Reason Institute, had this reaction to Greeley's pronouncement:

> Some liberal American Catholics, like Fr. Andrew Greeley, chose deliberately to misunderstand then-Cardinal Ratzinger's directive about voting for pro-abortion Catholics only for "proportionate reasons." Democrats and their hangers-on tried to spin this as meaning if they were good for "the poor," meaning they passed out other people's money, they had equal moral footing. In fact, as anyone who follows these issues in the Church knows, proportionate reasons means serious of-

fenses against life such as a massacre or genocide, and
even then abortion is killing 1.2 million Americans
alone a year, so it would have to be a rather large massacre or genocide intended by some pro-life Republicans that would explode their moral superiority on
abortion per se.

Similarly, in 2008, expect Giuliani partisans to zero in on this
sentence in the Bishops' statement to rationalize a vote for
Rudy: "There may be times when a Catholic who rejects a candidate's unacceptable position may decide to vote for that candidate for other morally grave reasons."

A Nov. 15 *New York Times* article laid the groundwork for
exploitation with this headline: "Catholic Bishops Offer Voting
Guide, Allowing Some Flexibility on Issue of Abortion." The
article quoted liberal theologian Thomas J. Reese, who when
asked, "Can a Catholic in good conscience vote for a candidate
who is pro-choice?" said "What [the Bishops] are saying is,
'Yes.'"

If Giuliani is the Republican presidential nominee, to carry
the closely contested swing states of Ohio, Pennsylvania, Missouri, and Wisconsin he will have to receive the support of a
key voting bloc – practicing Catholics.

To achieve this end, Giuliani's handlers will make sure that
Rudy, whose third marriage is outside the church, avoids alien-
ating Catholics by not receiving Holy Communion at Mass.
And since his extreme pro-abortion paper trail cannot be erad-
icated, his supporters might use the Bishops' statement as the
basis for portraying Giuliani as the lesser of two evils.

They could argue the Brooklyn-born Italian is really "one
of them" because, proportionally, Giuliani is much more in
tune with the basic values cherished by Catholics than his
Democratic opponent.

Anyone who suggests that Catholics should give Rudy a
pass based on "proportional reasoning" is wrong.

Because the sole intention of abortion is to take innocent
human life, it is by its nature intrinsically evil and can never be

on the same moral plane as the issues of poverty or health care or the war on terrorism.

Even the late Cardinal Joseph Bernadin, the leading proponent of the "seamless garment" argument, agreed that all issues do not have the same moral weight. In his sermon on Respect Life Sunday 1989, Cardinal Bernadin made this very clear:

> Not all values, however, are of equal weight. Some are more fundamental than others. On this Respect Life Sunday, I wish to emphasize that no earthly value is more fundamental than human life itself. Human life is the condition for enjoying freedom and all other values. Consequently, if one must choose between protecting or serving lesser human values that depend upon life for their existence and life itself, human life must take precedence. Today the recognition of human life as a fundamental value is threatened. Nowhere is this clearer than in the case of elective abortion. At present in our country this procedure takes the lives of over 4,000 unborn children every day and over 1.5 million each year.

To Giuliani supporters, a word to the wise: Don't try to use the Bishops' statement to rationalize a vote for Giuliani in 2008. Don't insult conscientious Catholics who know it is a grave public scandal for presidential contender Rudy Giuliani, a baptized Catholic, to condone the taking of innocent human life.

February 3, 2008

Why Giuliani Lost

The claim that Rudy Giuliani's misguided primary strategy was responsible for his presidential campaign's demise is wrong.

Giuliani went down because rank and file Republicans soured on him after they learned about his very liberal positions on social issues, his messy personal life, and his questionable business associates and clients.

Last year Rudy was riding high in the national polls and raised millions of dollars in red states like South Carolina and Florida thanks to his celebrity status. Scores of rich people lined up to plop down $2,300 to be photographed with "America's mayor." (Compared to those who paid $100,000 to hear Rudy's canned leadership speech, $2,300 was a bargain.) Traveling with Giuliani, *The Wall Street Journal*'s Daniel Henninger concluded, "Giuliani didn't have supporters; he had fans."

Celebrity Rudy also received plenty of help from neo-conservatives. They pounded away in op-ed pieces and on talk shows that the "Italian Stallion" was the right guy for the GOP despite his leftist pro-abortion, pro-gay rights and anti-gun positions. And by late summer, Washington's GOP establishment and media moguls began to fall for the neo-conservative contention that Giuliani was the inevitable nominee.

However, what the New York neo-cons and the D.C. crowd missed or ignored were public opinion polls that consistently indicated that the vast majority of Republicans did not know in the summer and fall that Giuliani was a thrice-married social liberal.

Giuliani's campaign began to unravel in December 2007 when the base of the Republican Party finally focused on his heavy political baggage. NBC's Tim Russert deserves the credit for getting their attention. Asking Giuliani on his Sunday "Meet the Press" program if it was appropriate for Secret Service agents to guard a president's mistress dumbstruck millions of Republicans. Iowa's senior senator, Chuck Grassley, spoke for many Republicans when he said "The New York lifestyle hasn't gone over [in] some places. It seems like the more people got acquainted with [Giuliani] the less they liked him."

Giuliani received only 2 percent of the South Carolina primary vote because his liberal record caught up with him. The millions he raised in Greenville and Spartanburg did not translate into votes. Ditto Florida.

Celebrity status and a well-heeled campaign treasury does not guarantee victory. Giuliani spent north of $50 million to win one delegate. (This breaks John Connolly's 1980 spending record of $12 million for one GOP delegate.)

Republican consultant Nelson Warfield best described the Giuliani candidacy: "It bordered on science fiction to think that someone as liberal on as many issues as Rudy Giuliani could become the Republican nominee. Rudy didn't even care enough about conservatives to lie to us. The problem wasn't the calendar; it was the candidate."

While Wall Street and country club Republicans control campaign money, Giuliani's failed candidacy proved that socially conservative Main Street and Wal-Mart Republicans control the outcome of primaries.

January 14, 2009

The Sorority Rules for Caroline

Manhattan's feminists are ecstatic that one of their leading so-
cialites, Caroline Kennedy, has declared she's available to fill
Hillary Clinton's soon-to-be-vacated U.S. Senate seat.
Kennedy's thin resume (she's chaired plenty of charity events),
her refusal to release her finances, and her universally ridiculed
public interviews have not dampened the enthusiasm of chic
leftists who are pressuring Governor David Paterson to ap-
point her.

In softball Q&As with New York's major newspapers (e.g.,
"What would your mother think of your candidacy?"),
Kennedy's utterances on public policy issues were downright
embarrassing. She was incapable of extending her remarks beyond the level of shallow Hamptons cocktail party chatter.

During the 41-minute *New York Post* interview, Kennedy
used the phrase "you know" 235 times. *The New York Times*
8,500-word transcript of Kennedy's sit-down contained 144
"you knows." Take a gander at her rambling explanation on
why she should be selected for the senate:

> I think this is about the future, and, um, *you know*, that's
> what I want to talk about, which is, what's going on in
> our state, *you know*, why I would be the best person to
> help deliver for New York. We're facing, *you know*, an
> economic crisis, the paper this morning said there's, *you
> know*, five billion dollars of construction projects which
> just stopped, *you know*, that's, *you know* – conversations
> a year ago, that's – beside that, I don't, as I said, I have
> conversations with a lot of people, and those are confi-
> dential.

To counter the mounting criticism and ridicule, the professional
feminists have been working overtime. The acerbic *Times*
columnist, Maureen Dowd, feigned humility saying "I know
about 'you knows,' I use that verbal crutch myself, a bad habit

that develops from shyness and reticence about public speaking." Outraged that the public wasn't rushing to embrace Caroline, Dowd complained, "People are suddenly awfully choosy about who gets to go to the former home of Jesse Helms, Strom Thurmond, and Robert Torricelli."

Kelli Conlin, head of NARAL Pro-Choice N.Y., defending Kennedy's lackluster public persona said, "I am dismayed at the uneven and entirely predictable treatment of Caroline and too many women who seek political office. Their experience is discounted, their skills ignored, their connections derided and their motives questioned."

Compare this supportive rhetoric to the vicious, shabby insults feminists hurled at Governor Sarah Palin throughout last fall's presidential campaign.

Palin, who proved herself in the political arena as an *elected* city councilman, mayor, and governor - whose vice presidential acceptance speech wowed the nation - who held her own in debate against Joe Biden - was not hailed by the women's movement as a heroine but derided as a bimbo, a hick, and a toned-down version of a porn actress.

Why is the political neophyte Kennedy treated differently than the political veteran Palin? Answer: Abortion.

Caroline Kennedy carries on her family's pro-abortion tradition. And nothing pleases the feminists more than a *Roe v. Wade* fan who is a baptized Catholic. Lest we forget, the Catholic pro-abortion movement was hatched at the Kennedy compound in Hyannis Port. In the summer of 1964, Bobby and Ted Kennedy met at the Cape with the nation's leading dissident Catholic clerics – Robert Drinan, Richard McCormick, Joseph Fuchs, and Charles Curran – to figure out how Catholic politicians could pander to the growing abortion movement without upsetting their Catholic constituencies. According to one witness, the theologians "concurred on certain basics . . . that a Catholic politician could in good conscience vote in favor of abortion." The action plan developed that week in Hyannis Port, in sociologist Anne Hendershott's judgment, contributed to effectively neutralizing the Catholic laity and "helped build the foundation for the [Democratic] party's reincarnation as the party of abortion."

Sarah Palin, on the other hand, was despised by the feminists because she broke their sorority rules: Palin defends life, opposes partial birth abortion, dared to have five children, and refused to terminate the life of her Down syndrome baby.

In a recent interview, Palin admitted the one lesson she learned in 2008 was that extremist feminists observe no rules of conduct when they come up against a public woman on the right who must be taken seriously. To accomplish their mission of destruction, lies, slander, and character assassination are acceptable tactics.

Palin also wondered how Caroline Kennedy will be treated and "if she will be handled with kid gloves or if she will be under a microscope." She also said, "as we watch we will perhaps be able to prove that there is a class issue here, also that was such a factor in the scrutiny of my candidacy versus, say, the scrutiny of what her candidacy may be."

Class issue? That's only part of the explanation for the draft-Kennedy movement. The primary reason both Manhattan's ritzy East Side and Trotskyite West Side feminists are "Sweet on Caroline" is that they are certain she will never violate their most sacred tenet: unlimited access to abortion.

May 3, 2010

Not-So-Fun City

The Museum of the City of New York will open an exhibit tomorrow called "America's Mayor: John V. Lindsay and the Reinvention of New York." It celebrates his "efforts to lead a city that was undergoing radical changes and that was the center of the upheavals of the 1960s and 1970s."

During his mayoral tenure (1966–1973), Lindsay presided over changes, all right – changes that ran the city into the ground: fiscally, economically and culturally. Any lessons to be learned, from the exhibit and from his mayoralty, should focus on what not to do.

John Vliet Lindsay (1921–2000) was born on West End Avenue, prepped at New Hampshire's St. Paul's School, graduated from Yale in 1943, served in the Navy and upon return to civilian life, graduated from Yale Law School. The 6'3" blond, blue-eyed Lindsay was elected in 1958 to represent Manhattan's Upper East Side "Silk Stocking" congressional district.

As the Republican-Liberal "fusion" candidate for mayor in 1965, Lindsay stated that he would "get as far away from the Republican Party as possible," even agreeing to give the Liberal Party one third of all city jobs and judgeships.

The fledging New York Conservative Party nominated another Yale graduate, William F. Buckley Jr., as its candidate for mayor. Buckley charmed New Yorkers with his roguish wit and intellectual depth and drove the humorless Lindsay crazy.

Lindsay retaliated by employing typical liberal smear tactics, falsely calling Buckley a "Goldwater racist" who adhered to "a radical philosophy full of hatred and division and violence."

Lindsay managed to win, but with only a 45 percent plurality.

In Lindsay's first minutes in office, the Transit Workers Union called the first mass-transit strike in city history. It would be a test of the new mayor's mettle, and the politically naive Lindsay failed – mostly because he approached the unions and their working-class members with an attitude of *noblesse oblige*.

Lindsay and his coterie of Upper East Side Boy Scouts had no clue about how New York City actually worked. Lindsay staffer Nancy Seifer noted the realization: "There was a whole world out there that nobody at City Hall knew anything about . . . If you didn't live on Central Park West, you were some kind of a lesser being."

While Lindsay deserves credit for calming the city during the '67 and '68 riots, he nevertheless had the knee-jerk reaction that the cause of the disorder was white racism. As vice chairman of President Johnson's Kerner Commission on Civil Disorders, Lindsay was responsible for the introductory statement in the commission's final report: "Our Nation is moving toward two societies, one black, one white – separate and unequal."

When Lindsay left office in December 1973, New Yorkers lived in a seriously declining city. As liberal journalist Murray Kempton observed: "[U]nder Lindsay, the air is fouler, the streets dirtier, the bicycle thieves more vigilant, the labor contracts more abandoned in their disregard for the public good, the Board of Education more dedicated to the manufacture of illiteracy than any of these elements ever were under Wagner." And another liberal, Jack Newfield, quipped that Lindsay "gave good intentions a bad name."

Lindsay's greatest mayoral "legacy" was his social-welfare spending spree. In 1960, 4 percent of the population received welfare benefits. That number had doubled by 1965 and by 1969 had grown to 13 percent. Expenditures for welfare programs rose from $400 million in 1965 to more than $1 billion by the end of Lindsay's first term. It became so easy to apply for welfare benefits that the *Daily News* called Lindsay's welfare commissioner "Come and Get It Ginsburg."

To pay for his spending spree, Lindsay used every imaginable financial gimmick. He increased nuisance taxes, water rates and sewer taxes and instituted the city income tax. In 1969, Budget Director Fred Hayes admitted: "We're going broke on $6.6 billion a year."

All the budgetary tricks, phantom revenues and capitalizing of expenses led to a situation in which 56 percent of locally raised taxes went either to debt service or to pension and welfare payments. Short-term debt, which in 1965 was $536 million, ballooned to $4.5 billion – 36 percent of total debt. By 1976, these abuses caused the financial markets to close their doors to the city and the state to take over the city's finances, complete with a default-on-debt decree from the state legislature.

"The rollovers, false revenue estimates and plain lies," journalist Ken Auletta wrote, "have robbed taxpayers of literally billions through excessive borrowings to cover up excessive fraud."

Mayor Lindsay proved that big, expensive, activist government not only failed to achieve expected social and financial equality but also created a permanent underclass – *and* bankrupted the nation's largest city.

President Obama, who is attempting to do the same on a national level, should take heed.

Chapter 5

Religion, Politics, and Science

July 23, 2008

Senator Barack Obama: Religion in the Public Square Is OK

For decades, many Catholic politicians rationalized their pro-abortion position by claiming that while they personally opposed abortion they could not impose their moral beliefs on others. To question this position publicly was tantamount to committing treason.

In 1984, for instance, all hell broke loose when New York's archbishop, John Cardinal O'Connor, commenting on the pro-abortion views of Democratic vice presidential nominee Geraldine Ferraro, said, "I do not see how a Catholic in good conscience can vote for an individual expressing himself or herself favoring abortion." Reacting to the archbishop's statement, *The New York Times* complained: "It might as well be said bluntly: . . . the effort to impose a religious test on the performance of Catholic politicians threatens the hard-won understanding that finally brought America to elect a Catholic president a generation ago."

Mario Cuomo, Tip O'Neill, Ted Kennedy, and others came to Ferraro's defense: Cuomo delivered a now infamous address at the University of Notre Dame defending the "I-personally-oppose-but . . ." position. Senator Kennedy accused Archbishop O'Connor of "blatant sectarian appeals" and argued that not "every moral command" could become law.

Twenty years later, John Kerry – the first baptized Catholic to be the presidential nominee of a major party since 1960 – employed the same old arguments to mask his pro-abortion views. Kerry told *The Washington Post* that "I oppose abortion . . . I believe life does begin at conception. [But] I can't take my Catholic belief, my article of faith and legislate it on a Protestant or Jew or an atheist." The fact that defending innocent life is not merely some obscure Catholic dogma, or that Protestants, Jews, and some atheists, along with various others, also found abortion morally repugnant and a grave departure from core Western values has never seemed to register with Kerry and many Catholics like him.

In the second debate, when asked by a town hall participant how he can support federally financed abortions, he reaffirmed that stand claiming that even though he is a "practicing" Catholic, he had no choice but to support pro-abortion legislation because, "I can't take what is an article of faith for me and legislate it for someone who doesn't share that article of faith." In the third presidential debate – more of the same. When asked about Catholic bishops' comments on the potential sinfulness of voting for a pro-abortion, pro-unlimited stem cell research candidate, Kerry replied:

> I respect their views. I completely respect their views. I am a Catholic. And I grew up learning how to respect those views. But I disagree with them, as do many. I believe that I can't legislate or transfer to another American citizen my article of faith. What is an article of faith for me is not something that I can legislate on somebody who doesn't share that article of faith. I believe that choice, a woman's choice is between a woman, God and her doctor. And that's why I support that. Now I will not allow somebody to come in and change *Roe v. Wade*.

This deliberate muddling of a natural law protection of the unborn with an allegedly sectarian Catholic position, which cannot withstand a second's thought, still lives large among Democrats. But this year's presidential abortion debate may be different because the Democratic nominee, Senator Barack Obama, appears to reject the position of party elders that moral principles are an imposition on the body politic. As he said in a 2004 speech: "Secularists are wrong when they ask believers to leave their religion at the door before entering into the public square. Frederick Douglass, Abraham Lincoln, William Jennings Bryan, Dorothy Day, Martin Luther King – indeed, the majority of great reformers in American history – were not only motivated by faith, but repeatedly used religious language to argue for their cause. To say that men and women should not inject their 'personal morality' into public policy debates is a practical absurdity. Our law is by definition a codification of morality, much of it grounded in the Judeo-Christian tradition."

Obama is absolutely right. Every issue by its nature has a moral dimension. And to suggest that one can't vote one's conscience on important issues is morally and intellectually incoherent – for both politicians and ordinary voters. Every vote in favor of any piece of legislation requires an act of faith that it is the best policy to impose on all the American people – including those who don't share the legislator's views on the issue.

How Obama will publicly reconcile his Christian faith with his extremist pro-abortion positions without the "I can't impose" cover remains to be seen. Nevertheless, Obama's acknowledgment that the American republic will not be endangered if religious views are articulated in the political arena is a significant concession that practicing Catholics should not let him or his party forget.

March 10, 2009

Lincoln v. Obama on Catholic Consciences

In the weeks before the Lincoln Bicentennial, Americans were inundated with books, articles, commentary, and television programs praising our sixteenth president. Barack Obama – a Lincoln enthusiast – traveled to his inauguration via the same rail route Lincoln took in 1861, was sworn in with his hand on Lincoln's bible, and led the February 12 festivities. At commemoration speeches in Springfield, Illinois, and the District of Columbia, Obama made it clear that Lincoln is his model president.

Noticeably absent, however, was a discussion of Lincoln's relationship with American Catholics, their church, and issues that affected their lives. Obama might want to take a break from signing death warrants for embryos and other alleged acts of compassion, and familiarize himself with this piece of American history.

In 1844, the anti-Catholic nativist movement was in full swing. To bolster the presidential candidacy of Henry Clay, Daniel Webster called for the Whigs to adopt "an efficient reformation of the naturalization laws" and urged his party to align with the anti-Catholic nativists. Not all the Whigs went along. On June 12, 1844, at a Whig gathering in Springfield, Lincoln broke with his party and proposed:

> Resolved, That the *guarantee of the rights of conscience*, as found in our Constitution, is most sacred and inviolable, and one that belongs no less to the Catholic, than to the Protestant; and that all attempts to abridge or interfere with these rights, either of Catholic or Protestant, directly or indirectly, have our decided disapprobation, and shall ever have our most effective opposition.

A decade later, the fledging Republican Party was tempted to court the anti-Catholic Know-Nothings to patch together a winning coalition. Lincoln fearlessly repudiated this electoral strategy. In an 1855 letter to Joshua Speed, he explained:

> I am not a Know-Nothing. This is certain. How could I be? . . . As a nation, we began by declaring that *"all men are created equal."* We now practically read it "all men are created equal, *except negroes."* When the Know-Nothings get control, it will read "all men are created equal, except negroes, *and foreigners, and Catholics."* When it comes to this I should prefer emigrating to some country where they make no pretence of loving liberty – to Russia, for instance, where despotism can be taken pure, and without the base alloy of hypocrisy.

When the Republicans met in 1860 for their nominating convention, Lincoln knew that party zealots had made countless pronouncements during the past four years promoting policies that alienated the Catholic population. In 1859, for instance, the Republican-controlled Massachusetts legislature called for a state constitutional amendment to extend the waiting time before newly naturalized citizens could vote, which infuriated Catholics.

Lincoln forcefully opposed the Massachusetts voting law: "I am against its adoption, not only in Illinois, but in every other place in which I have the right to oppose it. . . . It is well known that I deplore the oppressed condition of the blacks, and it would, therefore, be very inconsistent for me to look with approval upon any measure that infringes upon the inalienable rights of white men, whether or not they are born in another land or speak a different language from our own."

When the Civil War commenced, Catholics could be objective about grandstanding on both sides: almost none were slave owners or proprietors of northern manufacturing plants who viewed slavery as an unfair labor advantage. Despite the political contradictions and hypocrisy, most Irish Catholics in the North agreed to fight to preserve the Union at all costs. German Catholics in Pennsylvania and the Midwest fought because they staunchly opposed slavery and its extension into new territories.

In 1863, riots broke out in New York because a disproportionately high number of men were drafted in heavily Catholic congressional districts compared to the Protestant-dominated upstate districts. Lincoln was grateful that Archbishop John Hughes quelled the outbreaks. Speaking to thousands of his flock outside his residence, the ailing shepherd asserted, "A man has a right to defend his shanty, if it be no more, or his house, or his church at the risk of his life; but the cause must be always just, it must be defensive, not aggressive." After cheers and a final benediction, he sent the crowd home and they answered in unison, "We will."

Recognizing the importance of Catholic manpower in the Union Army – about 200,000 – and the influence of clergy on men in uniform, Lincoln began regularly consulting key bishops. He established an excellent relationship with Hughes, and before the archbishop died in 1864, President Lincoln asked him to handle delicate missions, once sending him to France as an unofficial State Department emissary. In return, Lincoln urged the Vatican to give Hughes the cardinal's red hat.

By the end of the Civil War, the Catholic Church's prestige was greatly enhanced. The Church remained unified; her soldiers fought bravely; and Americans witnessed uncountable acts of Catholic charity. The Daughters of Charity, the Sisters of Mercy, and other religious orders impressed the public with help to the wounded and distraught. Catholic and non-Catholic comrades, living, marching, and fighting together, dispelled many old prejudices.

Throughout his life, Lincoln held true to his conviction that government could never force persons to violate their consciences. He understood that these "laws of nature and nature's God" are the great guardians of the soul of democracy, which is the intrinsic value of the person. Without respect for personhood, the certitude that every man and woman matters, liberty becomes license and the responsibility to do what is right declines into the right to do what is irresponsible.

As President Obama contemplates rescinding conscience protection for Catholic health-care providers, thus forcing pro-life medical professionals to violate their moral convictions against taking innocent human life, he might reflect on his great predecessor's words and deeds. Like Lincoln, he might reach out to the Church hierarchy to hear how proposed policy changes infringe on the rights of Catholics to act according to their consciences. Because Honest Abe had it right: conscience "is most sacred and inviolable."

April 7, 2010

Obamacare and the Bishops

The American bishops had some tough going during the Obamacare debate. They caught lots of flak from media moguls on the left, congressional leaders, and renegade Catholics because they dared to inform their flocks that portions of the health care proposal violate Church teachings on the sanctity of human life.

Syndicated columnist E.J. Dionne, for instance, complained that the bishops were discarding "the flag of social justice" because they said the final bill was not abortion-neutral and undermined the Hyde Amendment, which prohibits using federal tax dollars to pay for abortion except in cases of rape and incest.

Speaker Nancy Pelosi, a baptized Catholic, insisted on advertising her ignorance of the Church's position regarding human freedom while dismissing the objections of the bishops: "I practically mourn the difference of opinion because I feel what I was raised to believe is consistent with what I profess, and that we are all endowed with a free will and a responsibility to answer for our actions. And that women should have the opportunity to exercise their free will." Pelosi, it seems, is blissfully and aggressively unaware that freedom is not an endorsement of bad moral choices. One must avoid immoral actions, such as abortion, that go against an informed Catholic conscience and simple natural law principles. Is she unaware or is there a more sinister explanation?

Then there were other Catholics who simply thumbed their noses at the bishops. The Catholic Health Association, a hospital trade group, endorsed the Senate health-care bill despite the abortion problem and the absence of language that would protect freedom of conscience for Catholics and other medical personnel. The Leadership Conference of Women Religious, a group of largely dissenting nuns, also broke ranks and supported the bill.

The New York Times and *The Washington Post* applauded these dissidents in front-page stories. Maureen Dowd, the *Times'* most prolific anti-Catholic polemicist, joyously proclaimed that "the nuns provided the Democrats with cover" to procure the last votes needed for House passage. She was right – 84 of the 93 Catholic House Democrats voted for passage. (All 37 Catholic Republicans opposed.)

The fact that the U.S. bishops have for a hundred years called "for reform of our healthcare system so that all may have access to the care that recognizes and affirms their human dignity" did not matter in the national debate. Because the bishops did not embrace, without question, a health-care agenda at variance with several basic American principles, they were portrayed as being out of touch, stepping over the line, and violating separation of church and state.

This line of attack is not new; it has been going on for decades. When New York's John Cardinal O'Connor said in 1984, "I do not see how a Catholic in good conscience can vote for an individual expressing himself or herself favoring abortion," the same crowd went ballistic. In an editorial, the *Times* took this shot at O'Connor: "It might as well be said bluntly . . . the effort to impose a religious test on the performance of Catholic politicians threatens the hard-won understanding that finally brought America to elect a Catholic president a generation ago." Senator Ted Kennedy accused O'Connor of "blatant sectarian appeals" and argued that not "every moral command" could become law.

In 2004, after distribution of Holy Communion was denied to several recalcitrant Catholic politicians, forty-eight pro-abortion Catholic members of Congress publicly complained that the "right to religious belief and separation of church and state" would be violated if the bishops insisted on enforcing this sanction. *The New York Times* supported the pols stating that "threats by some bishops to deny communion to Catholic politicians who support abortion rights" are "deeply hurtful." The *Times* went on to warn Catholic churchmen that "any attempt to make elected leaders toe a doctrinal line when it comes to their public duties raises multiple risks. Breaching the church-state line that is so necessary to protect religious freedom is one. Figuring out when to stop is another."

In other words, the bishops violate "separation of church and state" when they set rules about the worthiness of their *own* members to receive Holy Communion that the secular *Times* doesn't like. How ridiculous is that?

On the other hand, these critics apply a different set of rules to bishops when it involves positions they approve. In the 1960s, they lauded the bishop of New Orleans for excommunicating racist Catholics for opposing the civil rights movement. And liberals cheered when the bishops criticized President Ronald Reagan's nuclear and fiscal policies in "The Challenge of Peace" (1983) and "Economic Justice for All" (1986).

What these critics fail to grasp is that bishops, as shepherds, have a duty to their flocks to offer guidance on the Church's moral teachings. They also have an obligation to correct any person – especially any Catholic who is a highly visible public figure – who misleads or sows confusion about Church doctrine. Clergy of all faiths explain to their co-religionists how their religions apply in the temporal world. Catholics are no different.

Throughout the health-care debate, the U.S. Conference of Catholic Bishops, led by Chicago's Francis Cardinal George, acted forthrightly and courageously by insisting on reform that "truly protects the life, dignity, consciences, and health of all." But it was a rough patch, and after Obamacare kicks in it will probably get rougher, especially if the bishops are forced into a situation in which they conclude that the only way to uphold moral principles within Catholic institutions is for the Church to get out of the health-care business entirely.

And the pressures probably won't stop there.

September 23, 2009

ACORN's Problems – and the Church

ACORN, the radical community organizing group that receives tens of millions of taxpayers' money to promote victimology, has dominated the headlines this past week. In ACORN's Washington, Baltimore, and Brooklyn offices, employees were caught on hidden cameras counseling two undercover conservative activists, posing as a prostitute and a pimp, on how they can obtain a mortgage for a brothel. Said one loan counselor: "Honesty is not going to get you the house. . . . You can't say what you do for a living."

Shocked that ACORN – which was accused once again last year of voter registration fraud – flagrantly evades government rules and regulations, Congress froze their federal funding. Even America's number one community organizer who trained ACORN activists, President Obama, has turned his back on the organization.

No one should be surprised that ACORN – which has over 700 chapters in 50 cities – bends the law to ensure the "maximum eligible participation" of the downtrodden in the nation's largesse. They're merely following the strategy of their intellectual granddaddy – Saul Alinsky.

Alinsky (1909–1972), a Chicago rabble-rouser, appeared on the national radar screen in 1947 when his book *Reveille for Radicals* hit the bestseller list. Rejecting American liberalism and the labor union movement because they merely hoped to reform capitalism, Alinsky called for the training of professional revolutionaries to infiltrate cities and use "whatever works to get power to the people" in order "to advance from the jungle of laissez-faire capitalism . . . where the means of economic production will be owned by all of the people instead of just a comparative handful." His 1971 *Rules for Radicals: A Pragmatic Primer for Realistic Radicals*, shaped a whole generation of leftists now running America's social programs.

Described as an "organizer magician," Alinsky's role model

was "the first radical known to man who rebelled against the establishment and did it so effectively that he at least won his own kingdom – Lucifer." And to achieve desired political ends, Alinsky advised his followers to employ the tactics of intimidation: "Pick the target, freeze it, personalize it and polarize it. . . . Go after people and not institutions; people hurt faster than institutions. (This is cruel but very effective, direct, personalized criticism and ridicule works.)"

Alinsky influenced scores of leftists including Hillary Clinton and Barack Obama. As an undergraduate, Hillary Rodham met with Alinsky several times, declined a job offer from him, and wrote a ninety-two-page senior thesis, "There Is Only the Flight," that analyzed Alinsky's approach. Although the thesis has been sealed by Wellesley College, Mrs. Clinton has said publicly that Alinsky's "abrasive tactics paid off" and that her paper "basically argued that [Alinsky] was right."

As a Chicago community organizer, Obama taught the Alinsky method to ACORN agitators. His former supervisor, Gregory Galluzzo, who humbly calls himself Alinsky's St. Paul, claims that "Obama's exposure to [Alinsky's] liturgy taught him that wisdom can emerge from the grass roots."

All this was probably only to be expected. But when Alinsky began his career in the 1930s as an urban agitator in the Chicago stockyards neighborhoods known as "back of the yards," he also managed to strike an alliance with the Catholic Archdiocese of Chicago, which helped him found the community organizing operation, Industrial Areas Foundation (IAF), which to this day holds training workshops for aspiring radical activists.

Influential Catholics embraced Alinsky's politics of personal destruction. Then Chicago Auxiliary Bishop Bernard J. Sheil called *Reveille for Radicals* "a life-saving handbook for the salvation of democracy" and the great French Catholic philosopher Jacques Maritain called it "epoch making."

In the 1950s, Father John Egan of the Cana Conference, who

met Alinsky through Maritain, was so impressed with Alinsky's hands-on experience and confrontational style that he
convinced Chicago's Samuel Cardinal Stritch to hire IAF to advance social projects. According to Church historian Steven
Avella, Cardinal Stritch and his successor Albert Cardinal
Meyer funded Alinsky community organizing operations for
years because he persuaded them that the "Church could be a
very powerful social force in . . . Chicago if it could only mobi-
lize itself for action."

Alinsky trained scores of young priests who later took on
major responsibilities within the Church bureaucracy including
the U.S. Catholic Conference. Thomas Pauken, a former Director of Vista, a federal agency that gives grants to activist
groups, believes that "the radicalization of elements of the
Catholic clergy turned out to be one of Saul Alinsky's most significant accomplishments."

The "Great Society" war on poverty legislation codified
Alinsky's "rules for radicals" by calling for "maximum feasible
participation" of public agencies and non-profits in poor neighborhoods. This opened the floodgates for taxpayer, corporate,
and charity-funded community organizations like ACORN,
dedicated to implementing the Alinsky rule, "to rub the sores
of discontent."

Sadly, one "Great Society" inspired non-profit is the
Church-sponsored Campaign for Human Development
(CHD). Funded with millions of dollars dropped into Ameri-
can Catholic parish collection baskets, CHD donated over $100
million between 1972 and 1995 to Alinsky-type organizations.
The largest recipient was IAF. One-time CHD director, Father
Marvin Mottet, had worked as an ACORN organizer. In the
Fall of 2008, Campaign for Human Development suspended
all donations to ACORN after allegations that over $1 million
had been embezzled from that organization. According to the
Catholic News Service, in the previous decade CHD had given
approximately $7.3 million to ACORN.

Saul Alinsky's goal was to create "a backyard revolution in

cities across America." Little did he know that his revolution would advance far beyond Chicago's neighborhoods and bring corruption to the front steps of the White House – and the Catholic Church.

April 21, 2009

"Us vs. Them" Populism

Populism is back in fashion. A number of our leaders who despise the middle class and the values they hold are now urging folks to grab their pitchforks, take to the streets, and drive the money-changers and other undesirables out of town.

This is a different populism than was urged upon us in the recent past. One prominent convert to the new populism is liberal political columnist Tom Franks. In his 2004 book, *What's the Matter with Kansas?*, Franks vehemently opposed "us vs. them" populism when the "us" were social conservatives. Now he is cheering populists who created "bonus rage" by blowing the whistle on "them" – bankers, insurance executives, and anyone else deemed to be standing in the way of progressives.

In Baltimore recently, the Saul Alinsky-inspired group ACORN (Association of Community Organizations for Reform Now) – which could potentially receive billions from the Obama stimulus program to finance its activities – staged a mob takeover of a single-family home that was about to be repossessed.

There have been other reports of populist commotion. AIG executives and staff were threatened with strangulation by piano wire. Web sites have posted "Burn a Banker" advertisements.

Should Catholics be concerned about populist uprisings? Absolutely. Since the Age of Jackson, "us versus them" movements have aimed at resisting or destroying the nation's number one "them" – Roman Catholics. We have been the targets of numerous populist movements, including the anti-Masons, the Know-Nothings, the People's Party, and the Ku Klux Klan.

During the 1830s and 1840s, underground anti-Catholic movements led by back- alley, low-life bigots flared into full-fledged nativist populist crusades that came close to leaving major northern cities in shambles.

In August 1835, a Boston mob screaming "down with the

cross" torched an Ursuline convent and school dormitory and violated their graveyard. Anti-Catholic populist rage spread all over New England.

Pennsylvania nativists took to the streets in May 1844, attacked Philadelphia Bishop Patrick Kenrick, burnt St. Augustine's Church, an adjoining monastery, and a 5,000-book library.

The Know-Nothings marshalled lawless gangs who threatened Catholic voters on Election Day 1856. Baltimore, New Orleans, St. Louis, and numerous other cities reported violent clashes at the polls that often ended with dead bodies on the streets.

The 1890s rural People's Party populist movement, dedicated to the cause of the Anglo-Saxon "common man," viewed eastern urban America dominated by Catholics as enemy country. Their hero, William Jennings Bryan – three-time Democratic Party nominee for president – complained on the campaign trail that he was "tired of hearing about laws made for the benefit of men who work in shops." Bryan took a shot at Catholic immigration when he declared he was opposed to the "dumping of the criminal classes upon our shore." A Catholic priest in New York denounced Bryan from his pulpit as a "demagogue whose patriotism was all in his jawbone."

In the post-World War I era, a revamped, populist Ku Klux Klan took their racist, anti-Semitic, anti-Catholic platform national and recruited four million members. While their terrorist methods – lynchings, bombings, and arson – eventually discredited the Klan and led by 1929 to its rapid decline, in 1924 it was at the height of its power and forced itself upon that year's National Democratic Convention. To stick it in the eye of New York's governor, Alfred E. Smith, the first Catholic to have his name placed in nomination for the office of president of the United States, a vote rejecting condemnation of the Klan was passed by convention delegates.

Lots of Catholics believe all this came to an end with the election of John F. Kennedy to the presidency in 1960. For all his popular appeal, however, Kennedy had to all but renounce his faith in front of a room full of Protestant ministers in Houston to succeed.

It doesn't take a literary critic to detect the ways in which anti-Catholicism has covertly continued in American culture. The pro-abortion crowd, for example, has tried to paint pro-lifers as a Catholic clique, when in fact it is composed of Protestants, evangelicals, Orthodox Christians, Orthodox Jews, and even non-believers who just see abortion as wrong.

In a similar vein, Catholic priests are vilified as "pedophiles" and our bishops denounced as enablers, with some justice. But much higher percentages of public school teachers and child abusers in other professions go all but unremarked and even get special protections.

Today groups like ACORN could easily be persuaded by their funders to target their venom on Catholic core beliefs. Their membership could be mobilized to harass and intimidate Catholics who are pro-life and opposed to same-sex marriage. If you think this is farfetched, talk to anyone who's been active in opposing gay marriage. Lots of them have had to get unlisted numbers and endure threats.

California Christians who supported the victorious Proposition 8, which rejected the state court recognition of same-sex marriage, have been threatened and harassed by gay-marriage proponents. These zealots only like democracy when they win, which is not often when the case is put to a popular vote.

In the twenty-first century, practicing Catholics in the public square must realize that the level of bias against Catholicism remains very high. Catholics are still viewed by the secular humanists as, for all intents and purposes, public villains, and for them anti-Catholicism is still an acceptable prejudice. Hence, Catholics should be ever vigilant of secular populist causes fueled by what historian Richard Hofstadter called "absolutist enthusiasm."

July 26, 2010

The Family and the Social-Assistance State

The economic downturn has revealed staggering absurdities in the ways government regularly does business, including spectacular instances of high spending beyond available means in states like California – with no thought about inevitable rainy days. But the problems are compounded by a liberal media that misreads the signs of distress as lack of compassion rather than what they really are: indications of a subversion of a natural order.

Several weeks ago, newspapers in NYC started running stories about the ways in which the city's budget woes were causing cuts in child and elder care. In the process, they showed how much the government-run programs have replaced the natural institutions of neighborhood and family to the detriment of the latter.

Catholic teaching – indeed all sane social philosophy – has long regarded the family as the "original cell of social life." In *Centesimus Annus*, Pope John Paul II pointed out the dangers to the family from the "Social Assistance State," and the importance of subsidiarity in relief efforts, which he said should respect the proper authority of lower-order communities and should be as brief as possible in order to avoid creating a pernicious dependency. Most social scientists, of course, make light of this danger.

One social scientist who appreciated the Church's social doctrines on the family and understood the limits of social planning was the late Daniel Patrick Moynihan. For the record, I admired Moynihan the urban-policy expert, not the U.S. Senator. As a New York resident, I voted against him four times.

But during the heyday of President Lyndon Johnson's Great Society, when the federal government was writing blank checks for many hastily conceived and dubious social welfare programs, Assistant Secretary of Labor D. P. Moynihan issued a groundbreaking 1965 report, *The Negro Family: the Case for*

National Action. "The Moynihan Report," as it famously became known, was based on work by the Labor Department's Policy Planning and Research Staff. It painted a bleak picture of the nation's inner-city African-American poor.

Moynihan found that many poor blacks were caught up in a "tangle of pathology" thanks to U.S. welfare systems that simply "pensioned the Negros off." The expansion of Aid to Families with Dependent Children (AFDC) – which was originally created in 1935 to provide help to needy orphans and widows – actually encouraged black men to abandon their children because AFDC could not be paid to families where fathers were in the home. This also contributed to a sharp rise in out-of-wedlock black births.

Moynihan added that the absence of male figures damaged family stability and contributed to an "entire sub-culture of dependency, alienation, and despair." It also pushed black families into "a matriarchal structure, which, because it is so out of touch with the rest of American Society, seriously retards the progress of the group as a whole, and imposes a crushing burden on the Negro male and in consequence, on a great many Negro women as well."

Moynihan was brought up Catholic and lived in a fatherless home; he understood the importance of family, religious and neighborhood ties, and "the enduring power of ethnic and racial cultures." And he approached the problem of the disintegrating black family from a different perspective than was typical at the time.

Freedom Is Not Enough, a recently published book on the Moynihan Report by historian James T. Patterson, points out that Moynihan, influenced by "Catholic social welfare philosophy (which placed family well-being at the core of the good society) . . . favored enactment of family allowances that would be given to *all* families with children." He also argued for programs that would give "men proper jobs and a respectable place in the community and family."

All hell broke loose after President Johnson said a June 1965 commencement speech at Howard University ("Freedom Is Not Enough," based on Moynihan's findings) that if the black family unit did not become more cohesive, all the civil-rights gains would become meaningless.

Moynihan was assaulted by members of the Civil Rights Movement, the poverty industry, and the fledging feminist movement for his "unflattering description of matriarchy" and for leaving the "impression that lower-class black women having babies out of wedlock were irresponsible." Patricia Harris, a black leader, complained that the family issue was not *the* explanation for the problems of African-Americans. It was "white discrimination against them, the white assumption of black inferiority." Dr. Benjamin F. Payton, a black sociologist, denounced Moynihan as a "crypto-racist."

An intimidated Lyndon Johnson distanced himself from the speech; his administration repudiated the Moynihan Report; and their destructive poverty programs continued to be funded.

Despite the success of the 1996 federal welfare reform legislation (the Personal Responsibility and Work Opportunity Reconciliation Act), inner-city African-Americans are still suffering from the unintended consequences of Great Society policies. Out-of-wedlock black births, which were 17 percent in 1940 and 25 percent in 1965, hit 72 percent in 2007 – even as racism in American society sharply declined.

Big government has consistently failed to address the problems of poor and troubled families, white and black. And the reasons for its shortcomings were best expressed by Pope John Paul II in *Centesimus Annus*: "Malfunctions and defects in the Social Assistance State are the result of an inadequate understanding of the tasks proper to the State. . . . By intervening directly and depriving society of its responsibility, the Social Assistance State leads to a loss of human energies and an inordinate increase of public agencies, which are dominated more by bureaucratic ways of thinking than by concern for serving their clients."

We still have not learned this crucial lesson – crucial both for American society and poor families themselves. Indeed, we've now got an administration that has used the current economic downturn as an excuse for the very same fundamental error of failing to extend subsidiarity into many more sectors of society. As in the past, the results are not likely to be pretty.

April 3, 2009

On Religion & Liberalism

Alan Wolfe, director of the Boisi Center for Religion and American Public Life at Boston College, has for years been peddling the notion that most middle-class Americans who believe in God want to lead a good life (which they alone will define) and are opposed to applying moral convictions to public policy. They also hold, he asserts, that religious structures – i.e., church, synagogue, and less tangible formal arrangements – are not a requirement for belief. The late Richard John Neuhaus used to say that Wolfe strangely shows little interest in or knowledge of American religion for a person in his position. Wolfe's new book, *The Future of Liberalism*, confirms that judgment.

Wolfe has nothing new to say on the subject. He repeats the old liberal nostrum that one should be autonomous "to live your life on terms you establish," not exactly, you might think, the central vision for a center on religion and public life at a Jesuit university. Wolfe contends that liberals have been on the lam for forty years because they were afraid to be liberal – they were intimidated by extremists on the left and right. But thanks to Barack Obama, they are now in vogue and should be out on the hustings converting the masses.

For Wolfe, welfare-state liberalism permits people to be independent and mobile. To promote individual autonomy, the state should not hesitate to be notoriously illiberal by intruding in the economy and the bedroom. Generous welfare benefits and abortion on demand will free people to live life to the fullest.

To justify this creed, Wolfe turns to Immanuel Kant (1724–1804), who he claims "expresses ideas that every liberal ought to welcome."

In one sense, this is quite odd, because Kant, although the champion of individual sovereignty, also believes in a strict sense of duty. But Kant has become a hero to some liberals because they like how he relocates the sources of morality from the objective world around us (which he believes our intellects cannot really reach) to principles within our own minds. In Kant, this turn was intended to preserve morality in a scientific age; but in others' hands it degenerates into a denial of moral absolutes and a radical assertion of personal autonomy.

For Kant, a key word, repeated with heavy Germanic emphasis, is duty. And everyone who has studied philosophy has been taught the famous categorical imperative: "Act only according to that maxim by which you can at the same time will that it should become a universal law."

But at the same time Kant makes man autonomous, a being who prescribes laws to himself in a sense, not a participant in the natural law. Kant is therefore useful to thinkers like Wolfe because he indirectly provides a rationale for their fundamental belief that there are no absolute truths, no unconditional principles or laws. All becomes relative. The basis of democracy is the ever-changing push and pull of diverse individual opinions and tastes. As John Paul II and Benedict XVI have pointed out, many of our fellow citizens have come to believe that skepticism is the precondition for democracy. Beliefs in transcendent order, metaphysics, common law, a fixed human nature, and other customs and prescriptions must be replaced with concepts that make room for autonomous choices.

As for Wolfe's view of society, he denies that we are endowed by God with an appetite and inclination for social life, or that we form society by the demands and impulses of our rational nature working through free will. Instead, he takes a Hobbesian approach that society is an artificial product of human agreement. Wolfe says society is not "natural" or "divinely ordained" and that for liberals, "constraints are not imposed by authorities over which people have no control or shaped by traditions they cannot influence, they are established instead by people themselves through some form of consent or social contract. . . . Once we have left the state of nature, we require the existence of society."

By contrast, Catholic social doctrine regards the state as subject to a higher law, which compels judges and legislators to respect the inherent dignity of men by recognizing that government's powers are limited. Authority in a natural society cannot come from the individuals composing the society, but must come from the author of the natural law from which natural societies derive their existence – God. The Founding Fathers of the United States had a strong sense of that as well. Even Jefferson, the least pious of our founders, once said that no society had ever been governed without God, or can be.

Personal autonomy and a society based on nothing but human will have become the default settings for a certain kind of contemporary liberalism. The few people likely to read and agree with Alan Wolfe's *The Future of Liberalism* will find in it little new except a renewed hope in this empty vision, which is, by its very nature, destined to fall apart, sooner rather than later. But others might find at least one novelty here: is this the kind of leadership a major Catholic institution – Boston College – really intends to provide in an institute of religion and American public life?

February 11, 2010

The Truth about Life-or-Death Decisions

The January 26, 2010 Science section of *The New York Times* carried an article by St. Louis writer Alicia von Stamwitz titled "An Ill Father, a Life-or-Death Decision," which described her chilling hospital experience caring for her gravely ill father.

The patient was sixty-nine, suffered from bipolar alcoholism, had had two open-heart surgeries, several strokes, and couldn't speak. The attending physician further diagnosed that his liver was severely damaged from taking Lithium, his heart was weak, kidneys were failing, lungs were filling up with liquid, and a tube had to be inserted in his windpipe.

Ms. von Stamwitz was taken aback in a meeting with the doctor. Instead of receiving medical advice, she was asked if her father had a living will and had given her power of attorney. She wrote that when she said, yes, "Visibly relieved, [the doctor] looks me in the eye and gently but pointedly asks: 'Does your father want us to employ extreme measures . . . knowing that he is not likely to improve?'"

Instead of deciding for her father, she asked him to squeeze her hand if he wanted to be intubated again. The father didn't squeeze but firmly nodded his head, yes.

The reaction from the attending nurses also shook up von Stamwitz. One nurse, "grunts and rolls her eyes," and another mutters, "Oh brother, here we go again."

Ms. von Stamwitz confesses it would have been terribly wrong for her to stop treatments: "I supposed my father's decision was a mistake. But it was his decision to make, not mine. My role was to support my father no matter what, and to tell the truth, no matter how hard."

What is most distressing about the von Stamwitz narrative is the behavior of the medical professionals. The attitude they displayed has become commonplace since the U.S. Supreme Court in *Cruzan v. Director, Missouri Department of Health* (1990) ruled that artificially supplied food and liquids could be denied to patients who had cognitive disabilities regardless of whether they were conscious or unconscious.

To make it easier for doctors to follow the court decision, the American Medical Association revised its canon of ethics to read: "Even if the patient is not terminally ill or permanently unconscious, it is not unethical to discontinue all means of life-sustaining medical treatment [including food and fluids] in accordance with a proper substituted judgment or best interests analysis."

Sadly, many secularists have applauded this death-by-dehydration court decision. In *Rethinking Life and Death*, Peter Singer jubilantly wrote: "The lives of such patients are of no benefit to them, and so doctors may lawfully stop feeding them to end their lives. With this decision the law has ended its unthinking commitment to the preservation of human life that is a merely biological existence. . . . In doing so they have shifted the boundary between what is and what is not murder. . . . Now, conduct intended to end life is lawful."

Contrary to claims of the culture-of-death crowd, dehydration is not a "good death." It's one of the worst ways to die. Here's one physician's description of death by dehydration: "A conscious person would feel it [dehydration] just as you or I would. They will go into seizures. Their skin cracks, their tongue cracks, their lips crack. They may have nosebleeds because of the drying of the mucus membranes, and heaving and vomiting might ensue because of the drying out of the stomach lining. They feel the pangs of hunger and thirst. Imagine going one day without a glass of water! Death by dehydration takes ten to fourteen days. It is an extremely agonizing death."

Cognizant that many in the field of medicine are abandoning their Hippocratic Oath and recognizing the need to protect human dignity through feeding the sick, Pope John Paul II in March 2004 said the following to an international Congress convened to study the ethics of Life-Sustaining Treatments:

> I feel the duty to reaffirm strongly that the intrinsic
> value and personal dignity of every human being do

not change, no matter what the concrete circumstances of his or her life. *A man, even if seriously ill or disabled in the exercise of his highest functions, is and always will be a man,* and he will never become a "vegetable" or an "animal.

Even our brothers and sisters who find themselves in the clinical condition of a "vegetative state" retain their human dignity in all its fullness. The loving gaze of God the Father continues to fall upon them, acknowledging them as his sons and daughters, especially in need of help.

The Church understands the pressures people like Alicia von Stamwitz encounter in caring for their aging and sickly loved ones. Hence, the Church insists health officials have an obligation to promote and make accessible proper palliative care and should be dedicated to promoting a wide range of programs to improve the state of care for the ill and disabled. The chronically ill have the right to compassionate, humane, and medically indicated treatment and care to live with dignity until the moment of natural death.

May 20, 2010

Natural Law – and Neuroscience

Because we are made in the image of God, the Church teaches that by our very nature, we can govern ourselves and understand what is true and good. The Catechism defines this as the Natural Law, which "expresses the original moral sense which enables man to discern by reason the good and the evil, the truth and the lie." Notre Dame law professor Charles Rice has called natural law "a set of manufacturer's directions written into our nature so that we can discover through reason how we ought to act."

The standard formulation of natural law is this: do good and avoid evil. From culture to culture and from person to person, variations may occur in what is meant by "good," but there will be utter consistency in the imperative to seek the good. In the common way of understanding natural law, there are five basic, natural inclinations that we may know by the use of reason: to seek the good; to preserve oneself in existence; to preserve the species; to live in community; and to use intellect and will. From these basic inclinations, man applies natural law by means of further elaboration and prudence.

The natural moral law is not an exclusively Catholic thing. The ancient Greeks (Heraclitus, Sophocles, Plato, Aristotle), the Romans (Cicero, Seneca, Epictetus), and the great Jewish philosopher Moses Maimonides among others throughout history, all agreed that eternal norms are "written in our hearts," universal laws that establish order for man.

Alongside this long philosophical tradition, there have also been scores of secular ideologies that have rejected the divine nature of man and have tried to refute or deny that moral absolutes exist. Materialism in particular assumes that we are born amoral and are nothing more than beasts governed by instincts, impulses, or the environment because we are biologically or psychologically or economically determined. Hence, beliefs in a transcendent order, absolute truths, metaphysics, common law, and other customs and prescriptions must be replaced with concepts that are allegedly workable and efficient, i.e., materialistic.

This position, for example, permitted U.S. Supreme Court Justice Oliver Wendell Holmes to conclude that "truth was a majority vote of the nation that could lick all others." In other words, only superior forces make everything work; a majority's feelings determine truth, morals, and law. Public policy varies with the tastes of electorates and those in power.

It now appears, however, that those who subscribe to anti-natural law positions and worship at the altar of what they think is science-based rationality have a problem on their hands. Modern medical technology has demonstrated that an unborn child is indeed a human person. And now there is evidence in the new cognitive sciences that confirms what natural law proponents have been arguing for thousands of years: human beings exhibit a moral sense from birth.

Psychologist Paul Bloom of Yale University's Infant Cognition Center recently wrote in a *New York Times* magazine article that "with the help of well-designed experiments, you can see glimmers of moral thought, moral judgment, and moral feelings even in the first year of life. Some sense of good and evil seems to be bred in the bones."

Sound familiar? Dr. Bloom's discovery appears to be similar to St. Paul's, who taught that natural law resides in the hearts of all. Better yet, how about St. Thomas Aquinas who wrote in the *Summa Theologiae*, "The first principle in the practical reason is one founded on the nature of good, that good is that which all things seek after. . . . Hence this is the first principle of [natural] law, that good is to be done and pursued, and evil is to be avoided."

Bloom's studies conclude that, from day one, babies begin to learn and that they "not only distinguish morally good acts from morally bad ones: they also grasp the demands of justice – that a good act should meet with a positive response and a bad act with a negative one."

Experiments revealed that six- to ten- month-old babies favor helpful people to hindering people. They prefer nice people over mean people. Babies watching one-act morality puppet shows preferred the good guy to the bad guy.

The results of a battery of tests performed on infants support the existence of baby morality. According to Bloom, they "respond on a gut level. Indeed, if you watch the older babies during the experiments, they don't act like impassive judges – they tend to smile and clap during good events and frown, shake their heads and look sad during the naughty events."

Bloom concedes that a moral system must have a starting point and that it might very well begin in babies. He's right, there is a starting point – at creation – which Aquinas described as "nothing other than the light of understanding placed in us by God; through it we know what we must do and what we must avoid."

Good moral philosophy and, now, good neuroscience, too.

May 5, 2010

Dr. Death Takes Hollywood

Hollywood's sophisticated humanitarians are at it again – this time with "You Don't Know Jack," a movie that celebrates M.D. and assisted-suicide convict Jack Kevorkian. Starring Al Pacino, the HBO production portrays Kevorkian, who boasts 125 notches on his assisted-suicide syringe, as a compassionate man persecuted by a lunatic fringe that dares to hold human life sacred no matter how diminished its quality.

Kevorkian takes a polar opposite view to the Church's constant teaching that "God alone is the Lord of life from its beginning until its end: no one can under any circumstances claim for himself the right directly to destroy an innocent human being." He has claimed the right to end life and admitted in April to CNN's Anderson Cooper, "Anytime you interfere with a natural process you are playing God." He has also mocked Christianity saying "Had Christ died in my [assisted suicide] van with people around him who loved him [it] would have been far more dignified."

Here are a few facts about Kevorkian that the movie fails to mention:

∗ Labeled by his medical school classmates as "Dr. Death" (because his hobby was to photograph patients' retina blood vessels at the moment of death), Kevorkian urged that criminals waiting on death row be "used as human guinea pigs." Experiments on criminals, he claimed, would save the lives of innocent *animals* killed in the name of science.

∗ In a 1991 work entitled *Prescription Medicide: The Goodness of a Planned Death*, Kevorkian introduces the term "obitiatry," the practice of experimentation on living humans while they are under anesthesia and prior to medicide. Dr. Death states that his ultimate aim "is not simply to help suffering or doomed persons kill themselves – that is merely the first step. . . . [What]

I find most satisfying is the prospect of making possible the performance of invaluable experiments or other beneficial medical acts under conditions that this first unpleasant step can help establish – in a word, obitiatry."

∗ Kevorkian also calls for the creation of boards that would certify obitiatrists trained in medicide. He would establish zones within a given state for obitiatry headquarters and death clinics, plans eerily reminiscent of the Nazis' Charitable Foundations for Institutional Care.

∗ Kevorkian made his public debut in 1990, when, after a brief meeting with Janet Adkins (who was diagnosed to be in the early states of Alzheimer's disease), he agreed to aid her in committing suicide. Although reprimanded, he was not prosecuted because Michigan, unlike thirty-five other states, did not have a statue forbidding assisted suicide.

Since the reprimand did not stop him, the Michigan state legislature passed a restrictive law to curtail Kevorkian's activities. Indicted three times, he was not convicted because the prosecution failed to prove that he actually intended to help people kill themselves, and because Kevorkian successfully convinced the jury that his goal was "to relieve intolerable pain and suffering . . . to remedy their [i.e., the patients'] anguish, their torture."

Dr. Death's killing spree continued. Autopsies of his victims, however, have revealed that most were not terminally ill. Consider the following examples:

- Suicide #3, Marjorie Wantz: she had a history of suicide attempts and complained of pelvic pain, but the autopsy did not indicate the presence of a terminal disease.
- Suicide #29, Ruth Neuman: the coroner's office stated, "whatever they claim, she was not terminally ill."
- Suicide #35, Judith Curren: she was overweight, tired,

depressed, and her family had a history of domestic violence, but she did not have a terminal illness.

Dr. D.J. Dragovic, Oakland County Michigan's medical examiner, who performed autopsies on twenty-seven of Kevorkian's cases, said that "at least half had serious questions about being terminal," and only four or five he said, "had just weeks to live. . . . There were a lot of people physically incapacitated that could have lived for many months to many years."

The law finally caught up with Kevorkian in 1999 when a Michigan jury declared him guilty of second-degree homicide. The prosecutor proved that Thomas York, who was not physically capable of killing himself, was murdered by Kevorkian who administered the lethal injection. Kevorkian was sentenced to ten to twenty-five years in prison. The presiding judge said, "You were on bond to another judge when you committed this offense, you were not licensed to practice medicine when you committed this offense. . . . And you had the audacity to go on national television, show the world what you did and dare the legal system to stop you. Well, sir, consider yourself stopped."

Kevorkian was paroled in 2007 after serving eight years in prison. Since his release, he has been on the lecture circuit addressing adoring crowds at colleges throughout the nation. At the April 19 preview of "You Don't Know Jack" in New York's Ziegfeld Theater, he walked down the red carpet alongside Al Pacino to a standing ovation.

Dr. Kevorkian and his groupies look forward to the day when legislation becomes law that will abrogate the rights of patients in favor of decisions by the doctor or the state. Obamacare, which includes medical rationing to reduce Medicare's projected $50 trillion unfunded liability, will among other dubious benefits take the first step toward realizing that goal.

August 10, 2008

Pig and Man: Intellectual Equals?

In a July 31 *New York Times* column, Nicholas Kristof celebrated
the rapidly growing animal-rights movement. Kristof reported
that Spain has legalized ape rights; Austrians are pushing legislation that would define the chimpanzee as a person; the Harvard Law School offers an animal-rights course; and an
animal-rights referendum will appear on the California ballot
in November. Convinced that "our descendants will look back
on our factory farms with uncomprehending revulsion,"
Kristoff writes of his experience growing up on a farm in Oregon, "Our cattle, sheep, chickens and goats had individual personalities but not such interesting ones that it bothered me that
they might end up in a stew. Pigs were more troubling because
of their unforgettable characters and obvious intelligence. To
this day, when tucking into a pork chop, I always feel as if it is
my intellectual equal."

If this were merely a personal confession of imbecility, it
would be odd (equality with a pork chop?), but no odder than
many things that appear in America's self-styled newspaper of
record. But Kristoff's bad conscience has clouded his judgment
about a universal proposition: because man is a person who
possesses a mind, he is substantially different from the pig and
every other creature. Only man possesses reason, imagination,
creativity, and capacities for moral thought and aesthetic experience. In the old saying: a man can make a monkey of himself,
but no monkey can make a man of himself. It is man's mind,
not his body, that is made in the image and likeness of God and
gives him his true dignity. Materialists may (apparently without irony) deny the existence of mind as a reality essentially
different from matter, even though it obviously takes a mind
to deny the existence of mind, since only a mind can affirm or
deny anything.

Mortimer Adler was a powerful exponent of the truth that
human nature differs from other animal natures because only

man possesses "the related powers of propositional speech and conceptual thought," and because human action is not governed by instinct. Man is free to choose. "He has, in short, the power of self-determination, the power of creating or forming himself and his life according to his own decisions."

Man is an animal, to be sure (and often acts like one), but he is a very special animal, and it is this uniqueness that is the foundation of the "inalienable rights" referred to by Jefferson in the Declaration of Independence. Inalienable rights in the political sphere are rights that cannot justly be taken from citizens by the state, because they were not given by the state. Our inalienable rights come from God, the author of human nature, and no fact of birth, wealth, or social position merits or diminishes them. The liberties of the people are *natural* rights precisely because, as Jefferson put it, they are "the gift of God."

Most people do not know that the movement to equate man and beast is not new. The ideological origins of the animal-rights movement can be traced back to Cartesian reductionism, which measures the universe (mankind included) in exclusively material terms. As Descartes' contemporary Johannes Kepler (1571–1630) put it: "Nothing can be known except quantitatively." These thinkers rejected Aristotle's "Hylomorphism" which taught that man is composed of prime matter and substantial form (body and soul).

For Descartes and the later rationalists a man is not a person, he is a thing. "There is no difference between cabbages and kings," Nobel laureate Albert Szent Gyorgyi once quipped. "We are all recent leaves on the old tree of life." The supposed difference between man and beast, between for instance a saint and a pig, is merely a matter of degree.

This is completely alien to the classical notion, which defines the person as a "complete individual of intellectual nature" (Boethius). This view puts God and the angels together with man as persons, and, being non-reductive, excludes rodents. The *sine qua non* of the human person is the soul, which is not simply an extension of a material or animal nature. It was this unity of body and soul that led Thomas Aquinas to say that the human person "signifies what is most perfect in nature." With a soul, man has nobility. Without a soul, he has none.

If man is not exempt from the laws that govern beasts, he has no dignity, no inalienable rights, he is not a human person, he is a mere commodity. And if this notion prevails, abortion, euthanasia, assisted suicide, and cloning can be legally rationalized. If man is a non-person he can be deprived of life if "its" existence is inconvenient or deemed unfit by those holding judicial or legislative power.

The contemporary movement to elevate the beast is a ruse whose ultimate goal is to degrade man with a clear goal: implementing the culture of death.

ABOUT THE AUTHOR

George J. Marlin is a contributor to the New York Post, political columnist for the Long Island Business News, and a contributing editor of TheCatholicThing.com

He served two terms as Executive Director and CEO of the Port Authority of New York and New Jersey (1995–1997). In that capacity he managed thirty-five facilities, including the World Trade Center, La Guardia, JFK, and Newark Airports, PATH Subway and the four bridges and two tunnels that connect New York and New Jersey. In 1993, Mr. Marlin was the Conservative Party nominee for mayor of the City of New York. In 1994 he served on Governor-elect Pataki's transition team and in 2010 served on Governor-elect Andrew Cuomo's transition team. Mr. Marlin is a member of the Governor of New York's Council of Economic and Fiscal Advisors and a Director of the Nassau County Interim Finance Authority (NIFA), a fiscal oversight board.

Mr. Marlin is the author/editor of eleven books including *Squandered Opportunities: New York's Pataki Years; The American Catholic Voter: Two Hundred Years of Political Impact; Fighting the Good Fight: A History of the New York Conservative Party; The Guidebook to Municipal Bonds* (co-authored with Joe Mysak); *The Quotable Chesterton; Quotable Fulton Sheen;* and *Quotable Paul Johnson.* Mr. Marlin also serves as general editor of The Collected Works of G.K. Chesterton. His articles have appeared in *over two dozen periodicals, including The New York Times, National Review, Newsday, The Washington Times* and the *New York Daily News.* A lifelong resident of New York, Mr. Marlin resides with his wife, Barbara, in Nassau County.

INDEX